W9-BZB-923

24-Hour Knitting Projects

by Rita Weiss

Sterling Publishing Co., Inc.
New York

LIBRARY OF CONGRESS CATALOGING-IN-PUBLICATION DATA AVAILABLE

Weiss, Rita
    24-hour knitting projects / Rita Weiss.
        p.   cm.
    Includes index.
    ISBN 1-4027-1374-6
    1. Knitting—Patterns. I. Title: Twenty-four knitting projects.
    II. Title.

    TT825.W45423 2004
    746.43'20432—dc22   2004056594

                    2 4 6 8 10 9 7 5 3 1

Published by Sterling Publishing Co., Inc.
387 Park Avenue South, New York, NY 10016
© 2004 by The Creative Partners, LLC™
Distributed in Canada by Sterling Publishing
c/o Canadian Manda Group, 165 Dufferin Street
Toronto, Ontario, Canada M6K 3H6
Distributed in Great Britain by Chrysalis Books Group PLC
The Chrysalis Building, Bramley Road, London W10 6SP, England
Distributed in Australia by Capricorn Link (Australia) Pty. Ltd.
P.O. Box 704, Windsor, NSW 2756, Australia

Printed in China
All rights reserved

Sterling ISBN 1-4027-1374-6

Introduction

What are you planning for the next 24 hours?

Actually, 24 hours don't have to come all at once. They can be eight days of three hours, three eight-hour days, or 24 days of only one hour.

What are you going to do with that time? You could clean your closets, or visit your in-laws. Maybe you'd prefer taking a bus load of kids on a school field trip, or having some root canal work done?

If none of these possibilities appeals to you, why not try knitting?

Can't remember how to knit? Confused as to what those abbreviations and symbols mean? Spend a little time with our "Refresher Course" starting on page 119. Then join me on a walk through the pages of this book and select a sweater, a purse, an afghan, a scarf, or any of the other wonderful designs. Here are a wide variety of patterns that you can create in 24 hours or less to give as gifts or for your own enjoyment. Settle down with a cup of tea, a pair of knitting needles, some wonderful yarn, and let the rhythm of the stitches smooth away all your cares. Now isn't that a whole lot better than root canal?

Each pattern lists the amount of time it took my friends to finish a particular project. So if you have only an hour to complete your work, try making a "Snazzy Scarf" on page 40. If you have more time and want something a little more exciting, try the "Lion's Mane Evening Top" on page 16. That will almost fill up those 24 hours with purr-fect creativity.

Just remember that knitting shouldn't be a chore. If it takes longer than the suggested time to finish your project, that's all right too. There's no special award for the knitter who finishes first. So whether you finish in the allotted time or twice that time, the final result will be the same: a knitted project that you can display proudly.

Contents

MAKE A SPLASH
10

FUN AND FURRY
12

GLITTER AND GLITZ
14

LION'S MANE EVENING TOP
16

BOUCLÉ TOP
18

FORECAST FOR FALL
20

RIBBON FRINGE SCARF
22

POCKET SHAWL
24

YUMMY THROW
26

WEARIN' OF THE GREEN
28

VERY SUITABLE SWEATER
30

LET THE WINDS BLOW
32

BRIGHT AND BEAUTIFUL
34

DANCING DAYS
36

VESTED INTEREST
38

SNAZZY SCARVES
40

BOUDOIR AFGHAN
42

RAFFISH RAFFIA
44

SCARF OF MANY STYLES
46

SPORTY
48

ELEGANT BEADED SCARF
50

BEAUTIFUL IN BRONZE
52

SNAPPY SCRAPPY PURSE
54

JUST ENOUGH TOP
56

Gallery of Projects

MAKE A SPLASH

Designed by Sandy Scoville

Fashionable faux fur yarn accents a wonderful cropped top that goes everywhere in the summer. You're sure to make a fashion statement and a splash wherever you go.

PATTERN APPEARS ON PAGE 60

FUN AND FURRY

Designed by Susie Adams Steele

Wrap up in texture with this bright shoulder shawl accented with tassels. The lovely garment will not only garner attention but can be worn many ways, making it a great addition to any wardrobe.

PATTERN APPEARS ON PAGE 63

GLITTER AND GLITZ

Designed by Sandy Scoville

Be a shining star when you make an entrance in this glittering shawl and top. The silver metallic yarn adds the perfect glitter and glamour to this gorgeous outfit. The wearer will surely bask in the admiration.

PATTERN APPEARS ON PAGE 66

LION'S MANE EVENING TOP

Designed by Sandy Scoville

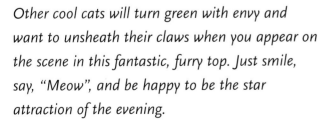

Other cool cats will turn green with envy and want to unsheath their claws when you appear on the scene in this fantastic, furry top. Just smile, say, "Meow", and be happy to be the star attraction of the evening.

PATTERN APPEARS ON PAGE 71

BOUCLÉ TOP

Designed by Sandy Scoville

No need for fancy stitches; gorgeous yarn is all you need to create this wonderfully stylish and warm pullover. The purple trim makes the perfect accent by highlighting the color and texture of the sweater.

PATTERN APPEARS ON PAGE 74

FORECAST FOR FALL

Designed by Sandy Scoville

Touches of colorful faux fur set off this wearable vest and its matching hat. When the weather starts to get nippy, wear this duo together or separately to expand your wardrobe.

PATTERN APPEARS ON PAGE 77

RIBBON FRINGE SCARF

Designed by Carol Wilson Mansfield

Ribbon fringe highlights the beautiful texture of this scarf, worked in a checkerboard pattern stitch that reflects the light while it keeps you warm and cozy in any kind of weather. Beauty and utility work hand in hand.

PATTERN APPEARS ON PAGE 82

POCKET SHAWL

Designed by Sandy Scoville

Warm hands mean warm hearts, the saying goes. Keep hearts warm with this warm and pretty shawl with deep pockets designed to keep hands warm on chilly days.

PATTERN APPEARS ON PAGE 84

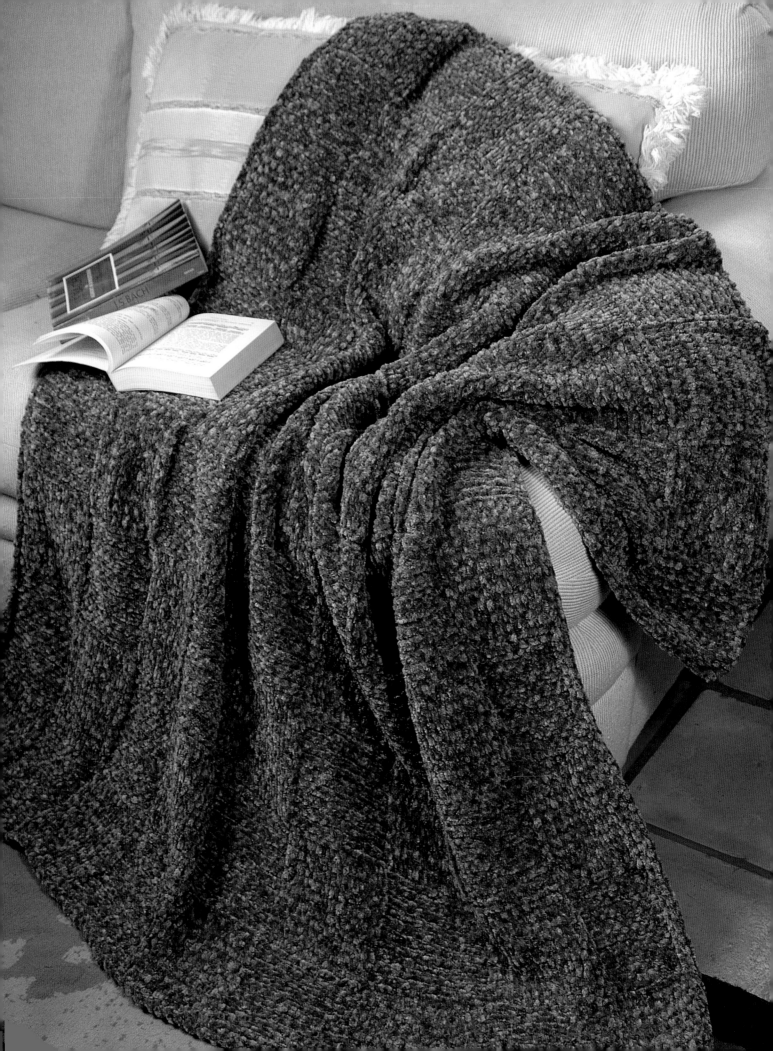

YUMMY THROW

Designed by Sandy Scoville

If you've always longed to wrap yourself in fur, this is your moment. Wrap yourself in this spectacular chenille throw that has the same feel and much of the same look as expensive fur.

PATTERN APPEARS ON PAGE 86

WEARIN' OF THE GREEN

Designed by Carol Wilson Mansfield

Let the March winds blow! When you've knitted this scarf and hat, you'll be certain that the wearer will not only be warm and comfortable but also the envy of all those fighting the cold.

PATTERN APPEARS ON PAGE 88

VERY SUITABLE SWEATER

Designed by Sandy Scoville

Jackets are back! The perfect blouse to wear under one is this sleeveless sweater; the lack of sleeves means that the sweater is comfortable under the jacket while its split turtleneck turns the sweater alone into a fashion statement.

PATTERN APPEARS ON PAGE 90

LET THE WINDS BLOW

What's not to love about this richly ribbed scarf that will snuggle up around your neck and keep out the threatening weather? You'll be smiling and perfectly comfy on your winter errands.

PATTERN APPEARS ON PAGE 92

BRIGHT AND BEAUTIFUL

Designed by Sandy Scoville

You'll love showing off your fashion flair with this colorful hat and scarf duo that are fun to make and fun to wear. Easy to use, the wonderful "eyelash" yarn makes the project look dramatic enough to turn heads in the marketplace.

PATTERN APPEARS ON PAGE 94

DANCING DAYS

Light and airy, this shawl will make you want to dance.
Quickly knitted, it's fun to wear. You'll feel like a famous movie
star on her way to a party steeped in admiring glances.

PATTERN APPEARS ON PAGE 96

VESTED INTEREST

Long and lovely, this simple vest shows off a beautiful yarn to perfection. It's knitted all in one piece with only two shoulder seams to sew. It's easy to make and simply wonderful.

PATTERN APPEARS ON PAGE 98

SNAZZY SCARVES

Fabulous fur scarves are now a fantastic fashion statement!
Make them in all colors to match your entire wardrobe.
Your needles will fly, and if you make a mistake,
it'll never show.

PATTERN APPEARS ON PAGE 100

BOUDOIR AFGHAN

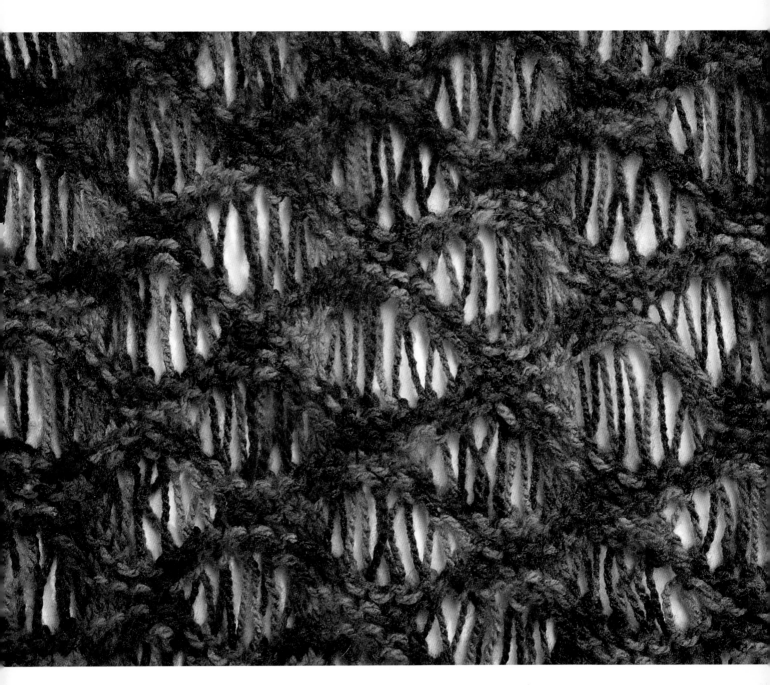

*Beautiful blue yarn combines with a lacy dropped
stitch to create a light but warm versatile afghan.
Just enough weight to keep you comfortable on
a cool summer evening.*

PATTERN APPEARS ON PAGE 102

RAFFISH RAFFIA

Designed by Kathleen Power Johnson

Raffia crafts an unusual purse with a tailored look and varied colors. The interesting cable moving up the bag adds dimension to this novel project.

PATTERN APPEARS ON PAGE 104

SCARF OF MANY STYLES

Designed by Sandy Scoville

Eye-popping color and textured yarn combine to make this a "wow" scarf that can be worn in many ways. Your mood will dictate the style. It will turn any garment into a fashion statement.

PATTERN APPEARS ON PAGE 106

SPORTY

Designed by Sandy Scoville

Top off your knitting skills with this rakish cap. Its jaunty look is sure to appeal to the dashing streak in everyone, and is the perfect touch to any wardrobe.

PATTERN APPEARS ON PAGE 108

ELEGANT BEADED SCARF

Designed by Carol Wilson Mansfield

The perfect addition to anyone's wardrobe is this elegant scarf created from a novelty printed yarn and garnished with a beaded trim. Transform any plain garment into a designer outfit.

PATTERN APPEARS ON PAGE 110

BEAUTIFUL IN BRONZE

Designed by Sandy Scoville

Where to wear it? Anywhere? Wear it on your shoulders. Wear it on your hips. It will always be admired.

PATTERN APPEARS ON PAGE 112

SNAPPY SCRAPPY PURSE

Designed by Sandy Scoville

A happy medley of fabulous textured yarns in go-anywhere colors makes this a must-have purse for every occasion. Deep enough to be really useful, it's secured with a fabulous button closure.

PATTERN APPEARS ON PAGE 114

JUST ENOUGH TOP

Designed by Sandy Scoville

Here's a sweater that's quick to make. Created in a bulky-weight ribbon type yarn, the garment has that extra bit of glamour. Finish the sweater with a row of fringe around the neck, and then don't be shy. Stand back for the compliments.

PATTERN APPEARS ON PAGE 116

Patterns

MAKE A SPLASH

Designed by Sandy Scoville

Note: *Instructions are written for size Small; changes for sizes Medium and Large are in parentheses.*

Size:	Small	Medium	Large
Body Chest Measurements:	32"–34"	34"–36"	36"–38"
Finished Chest Measurement:	34"	36"	38"

Time to make: About 17 hours

MATERIALS:

Worsted weight yarn, 7 (8, 9) oz purple; Novelty fur-type yarn, ½ oz (all sizes) blended reds and lavenders

Note: *Photographed model made with Bernat® So Soft®, Color #75330 Ultra Violet and Patons® Cha Cha, Color #02003 Be Bop.*

Size 8 (5 mm) knitting needles, or size required for gauge

Size 8 (5 mm) double-pointed knitting needles (for shoulder straps)

Sewing needle and matching thread

GAUGE:

9 sts = 2" in Stockinette Stitch (knit one row, purl one row.

Instructions:

BACK:

Starting at lower edge with purple, cast on 77 (81, 85) sts.

RIBBING:

Row 1 (right side)**:** K1; * P1, K1; rep from * across.

Row 2: P1; * K1, P1; rep from * across.

Rows 3 through 10: Rep Rows 1 and 2.

BODY:

Row 1 (right side): Purl.

Row 2: Inc (knit in front and back of first st), knit across: 78 (82, 86) sts.

Row 3: P2; * K2, P2; rep from * across.

Row 4: K2; * P2, K2; rep from * across.

Row 5: Purl.

Row 6: Knit.

Repeat Rows 3 through 6 until pieces measures about 11″ ending by working a Row 4.

UNDERARM AND BODICE SHAPING:

Row 1 (right side): Bind off first 6 sts; purl across.

Row 2: Bind off first 6 sts; knit across: 66 (70, 74) sts.

Row 3: Sl 1, K1, PSSO; K2; * P2, K2; rep from * to last 2 sts; K2 tog: 64 (68, 72) sts.

Row 4: P2 tog, K1; * P2, K2; rep from * to last 5 sts; P2, K1, P2 tog tbl: 62 (66, 70) sts.

Row 5: Sl 1, K1, PSSO; purl to last 2 sts; K2 tog: 60 (64, 68) sts.

Row 6: P2 tog, knit to last 2 sts; P2 tog tbl: 58 (62, 66) sts.

Rows 7 through 14 (14, 18): Rep Rows 3 through 6, 2 (2, 3) times: 42 (46, 42) sts.

Rows 15 (15, 19) through 16 (18, 20): Work in patt, dec at each end of every row. At end of last row: 38 (38, 38) sts.

Row 17 (19, 21): Work even in patt.

Bind off as to knit.

FRONT:

Work as for back for 16 (18, 20) rows of body.

Note: For front trim, carry purple loosely along wrong side.

Row 17 (19, 20): (right side): P20 (22, 24); join red, K4; with purple, purl rem sts.

Row 18 (20, 22): With purple, knit to first red st; with red, K4; with purple, knit rem sts.

Row 19 (21,23): With purple, work in patt to first red st; with red, P4; with purple, work in patt across.

Row 20 (22, 24): With purple, work in patt to first red st; with red, K4; with purple, work in patt across.

Rows 21 (23, 25) through 28 (30, 32): Rep Rows 19 (21, 23) and 20 (22, 24).

Cut red.

Rows 29 (31, 33) through 44 (46, 48):

61

continued on page 62

MAKE A SPLASH

continued

With purple, work in patt across.

Row 45: With purple, P58; join red, K4; with purple, purl across.

Row 46: With purple, knit to first red st; with red, K4; with purple, work in patt across.

Row 47: With purple, work in patt to first red st; with red, P4; with purple, work in patt across.

Row 48: With purple, work in patt to first red st; with red, K4; with purple, work in patt across.

Cut red.

With purple, work as for back through Row 17 (19, 21) of underarm and bodice shaping.

Cut purple.

TRIM:

Row 1 (right side)**:** With red, knit.

Row 2: Purl.

Row 3: Inc (knit in front and back of first st), knit to last st; inc: 40 sts.

Row 4: Purl.

Rows 5 through 10: Rep Rows 3 and 4. At end of Row 10: 46 sts. Bind off.

SHOULDER STRAP (make 2):
Note: Edges will come together at center back to form a flat tube.

With double pointed needles and purple, cast on 5 sts. Do not turn.

Row 1: K5; slide sts to opposite end of needle; do not turn.

Row 2: Carry yarn across wrong side of sts; knit. Slide sts to opposite end of needle; do not turn.

Rep Rows 1and 2 until strap measures 10" (all sizes).

Bind off.

FINISHING:
Sew side seams, carefully matching stitches.

Fold bodice trim forward and tack to bodice along side edges.

Sew shoulder straps to front and back.

FUN AND FURRY

Designed by Susie Adams Steele

Time to make: About 12 hours

SIZE:
One size fits all.

MATERIALS:
Novelty "fur" type yarn, 7 oz variegated
blues and greens
Worsted weight yarn, 1 oz green
for tassels
Note: *Photographed model made
with Crystal Palace Fizz, Color #7223
Seafoam and Bernat® Cottontots™,
Color #90712 Lime Berry.*
24" circular knitting needle, Size 9 (5 mm),
or size required for gauge

Size G (4 mm) crochet hook
Large stitch holder
Two ⅝" blue buttons with shanks
Sewing needle and matching thread
4 small safety pins

GAUGE:
18 sts = 4" in garter stitch (knit all rows)
20 rows = 2" (lay flat to measure)

Instructions:

BACK:
Beginning at lower back edge with fur yarn,
cast on one stitch; do not join. Work back
and forth in rows.

Row 1 (right side)**:** Inc (knit in front and
back of st): 2 sts.

Row 2: Inc in each st: 4 sts.

Row 3: Inc; knit to last st; inc: 6 sts.

Rows 4 through 47: Rep Row 3. At end of
Row 47: 94 sts.

Row 48: Inc; knit to last st; inc: 96 sts.

Row 49: Knit.

Rows 50 through 73: Rep Rows 48 and 49,
12 times more. At end of Row 73: 120 sts.

Mark beg and end of Row 73 with
safety pins.

continued on page 64

FUN AND FURRY
continued

SHOULDERS:
Continue in garter stitch until shoulders measure 7" from markers when lying flat; ending by working a wrong-side row.

DIVIDING ROW:
Row 1 (right side)**:** For Right Back Shoulder: K 50, put just knitted sts on stitch holder; for back neckline, bind off next 20 sts; for left back shoulder, K 50.

SHOULDER SHAPING:
Row 1 (wrong side)**:** Knit.

Rows 2 through 19: Knit.

Row 20 (right side)**:** K 50, for left front neckline, cast on 25 sts: 75 sts.

Rows 21 through 31: Knit.

LEFT FRONT:
Row 1 (right side)**:** Knit to last 2 sts; K2 tog: 74 sts.

Row 2: Knit.

Rows 3 through 22: Rep Rows 1 and 2, 10 times. At end of Row 22: 64 sts. Mark beg and end of Row 22.

Row 23: Sl 1, K1, PSSO; knit to last 2 sts; K2 tog: 62 sts.

Row 24: Knit.

Rep Rows 23 and 24 until 2 sts rem.

Last row: K2 tog.

Finish off.

RIGHT FRONT SHOULDER SHAPING:
Slip 50 sts from stitch holder onto needle; hold with wrong side facing.

Row 1 (wrong side)**:** Knit.

Rows 2 through 18: Knit.

Row 19: Knit; cast on 25 sts: 75 sts.

FRONT:
Rows 1 through 4: Knit.

Row 5 (buttonhole row)**:** K3, K2 tog, YO: buttonhole made; K17, K2 tog, YO: buttonhole made; knit rem sts.

Rows 6 through 10: Knit.

RIGHT FRONT:
Row 1 : Sl 1, K1, PSSO; knit rem sts: 74 sts.

Row 2: Knit.

Rows 3 through 22: Rep Rows 1 and 2. At end of Row 22: 64 sts.

Row 23: Sl 1, K1, PSSO; knit to last 2 sts; K2 tog: 62 sts.

Row 24: Knit.

Rep Rows 23 and 24 until 2 sts rem.

Next row: K2 tog.

Finish off.

NECKLINE EDGING:
Hold scarf with right side facing and left front neckline at top. With crochet hook, make a lp on hook, draw yarn through first cast-on neckline st; ch 1, sc in same st; working loosely around neckline, sc in each cast-on st, in edge of each row along left shoulder, in each bound-off st across back, in edge of each row along right shoulder,

and in each cast-on row along right front neckline.

Finish off. Weave in ends.

TASSEL (make three)
Cut 29, 9" lengths of lime green yarn for each tassel. Hold 27 strands tog; fold over 28th strand and tie that strand loosely to hold; wrap 29th strand tightly around folded strands about 1" below fold. Trim, leaving ends of 28th strand for attaching to scarf.

FINISHING:
Step 1: Fold right front over left front at neckline; mark for button placement opposite buttonholes. Sew buttons to left front.

Step 2: With loose ends, attach one tassel to front and back at lower points. Weave in ends.

GLITTER AND GLITZ SHAWL

Designed by Sandy Scoville

Time to make: About 23 hours

SIZE:

56" x 22"

MATERIALS:

Worsted weight yarn, 14 oz, silver.

Note: Photographed model made with Lion Brand Glitterspun, Color #150 Silver.

Size 11 (8 mm) knitting needles, or size required for gauge

Size I (5.5 mm) crochet hook

GAUGE:

14 sts = 4" in pattern stitch

Note: To check gauge: cast on 15 sts and work Rows 1 through 4. Repeat these 4 rows until swatch measures 4". Bind off. Swatch should measure 4" wide.

Instructions:

Cast on 75 sts.

Row 1 (right side)**:** K1; * YO, K2; rep from * across: 112 sts.

Row 2: P1; * P3, pass first of 3 sts just purled over 2 sts; rep from * across: 75 sts.

Row 3: K1; * K1, YO, K1; rep from * across: 112 sts.

Row 4: * P3, pass first of 3 sts just purled over 2 sts; rep from * to last st; P1: 75 sts.

Rep Rows 1 through 4 until shawl measures about 56", ending by working a wrong-side row.

Bind off loosely.

FRINGE:

Hold shawl with right side facing and short end of last row at top; with crochet hook, make lp on hook, join with an sc in first st; ch 1, * draw ch out to 10", insert hook in next st, draw up lp, YO and draw through lp and through l0" lp; draw long lp tight; ch 1; rep from * to last st; draw ch out to 10", insert hook in next st, draw up lp, YO and draw through lp and through 10" lp; ch 1. Finish off.

Weave in ends. Work fringe on opposite end in same manner, working in unused lps of beg ch.

GLITTER AND GLITZ BLOUSE

Designed by Sandy Scoville

Note: Instructions are written for size Small; changes for sizes Medium and Large are in parentheses.

Size:	Small	Medium	Large
Body Chest Measurements:	30″–32″	33″–34″	35″–36″
Finished Chest Measurement:	33″	35″	37″

Time to make: About 14 hours

MATERIALS:

Worsted weight yarn, 8 (8 3/4 , 9) oz, metallic silver

Note: Photographed model was made with Lion Brand Glitterspun, Color #150 Silver.

14″ straight knitting needles, size 7 (4.5 mm) or size required for gauge

2 large stitch holders

GAUGE:

5 sts = 1″ in Stockinette Stitch (knit one row, purl one row)

Instructions:

BACK:

Beginning at lower edge, cast on 77 (81, 85) sts.

BORDER:

Row 1 (right side)**:** Inc (knit in front and back of next st) in every st: 154 (162, 170) sts.

Row 2: K2 tog; * P2 tog; K2 tog; rep from * across: 77, (81, 85) sts.

Row 3: Rep Row 1.

Row 4: P2 tog; * K2 tog; P2 tog; rep from * across.

Rows 5 through 12: Rep Rows 1 through 4 twice more.

BODY:

Row 1: Knit.

Row 2: Purl.

Rows 3 through 10: Rep Rows 1 and 2.

Row 11: Inc (knit in front and back of next st); knit to last st; inc: 79 (83, 87) sts.

Row 12: Purl.

Rows 13 through 68: Rep Rows 5 through 12 in sequence 7 times more. At end of Row 68: 93 (97, 101) sts.

Rep Rows 1 and 2 until piece measures 9″ (9 1/2″, 10″) from cast-on row, ending by working a wrong-side row.

ARMHOLE SHAPING:

Row 1 (right side)**:** Bind off 5 sts; knit across.

Row 2: Bind off 5 sts; purl across: 83 (87, 91) sts.

Row 3: Knit.

Row 4: Purl.

Rep Rows 3 and 4 until armhole measures 6″ (6 1/2″, 7″), ending by working a wrong side row.

RIGHT BACK SHOULDER AND NECKLINE SHAPING:

Row 1 (right side)**:** K20 (21, 22); slip remaining sts onto cable needle.

Row 2: P1, P2 tog tbl; purl across: 19 (20, 21) sts

Row 3: Knit to last 3 sts; K2 tog; K1: 18 (19, 20) sts.

Rows 4 & 5: Rep Rows 2 and 3. At end of Row 5: 16 (17, 18) sts.

Row 6: Rep Row 2: 15 (16, 17) sts.

Row 7: Knit.

Row 8: Purl.

Rows 9 through 12: Rep Rows 7 and 8 twice.

Bind off.

LEFT SHOULDER AND NECKLINE SHAPING:
Hold back with right side facing, slip 20 (21, 22) sts at left arm edge onto knitting needle, leaving rem 43 (45, 47) sts at center on holder for neckline trim.

Row 1 (right side): Knit.

Row 2: Purl to last 3 sts; P2 tog; P1: 19 (20, 21) sts.

Row 3: K1, K2 tog tbl; knit across: 18 (19, 20) sts.

Rows 4 & 5: Rep Rows 2 and 3. At end of Row 5: 16 (17, 18) sts.

Row 6: Rep Row 2: 15 (16, 17) sts.

Row 7: Knit.

Row 8: Purl.

Rows 9 through 12: Rep Rows 7 and 8.

Bind off.

FRONT:
Work as for back through Row 4 of armhole shaping.

Rep Rows 3 & 4 until armhole measures 3" (4", 4½"): 83 (87, 91) sts.

LEFT FRONT SHOULDER AND NECKLINE SHAPING:
Row 1 (right side): K33 (34, 35) sts; slip remaining sts onto stitch holder.

Row 2: P1, P2 tog tbl; purl across: 32 (33, 34) sts.

Row 3: Knit to last 3 sts; K2 tog; K1: 31 (32, 33) sts.

Rows 4 through 19: Rep Rows 2 and 3, 8 times more. At end of Row 19: 15 (16, 17) sts.

Work even until left front measures same as back.

Bind off.

RIGHT FRONT SHOULDER AND NECKLINE SHAPING:
Hold front with right side facing, slip 33 (34, 35) sts at right edge from stitch holder onto needle; leave remaining 17 (19, 21) sts on holder for neckline trim.

Row 1 (right side): Knit.

Row 2: Purl to last 3 sts; P2 tog; P1: 32 (33, 34) sts.

Row 3: K1, K2 tog tbl; knit across: 31 (32, 33) sts.

Rows 4 through 19: Rep Rows 2 and 3. At

end of Row 19: 15 (16, 17) sts.

Bind off.

Sew left shoulder seam.

NECKLINE TRIM:
Note: Stitches may need to be added or subtracted to ensure that trim lies flat.

Row 1 (right side): Hold top with right side of back facing; starting in side of last row of right back shoulder and neckline shaping, pick up and knit 20 sts along neck edge to back stitch holder, move 43 (45, 47) sts from holder onto left needle, inc in each st: 86 (90, 94) sts; pick up and knit 20

69

continued on page 70

GLITTER AND GLITZ BLOUSE

continued

sts to shoulder seam; pick up and knit 40 sts to front stitch holder, move 17 (19, 21) sts from holder onto left needle, inc in each st: 34 (38, 42) sts; pick up 40 sts to last row of shoulder: 240 (248, 256) sts.

Row 2: * K2 tog; P2 tog; rep from * across: 120 (124, 128) sts.

Row 3: Inc (knit in front and back of next st) in each st.

Row 4: * P2 tog; K2 tog; rep from * across.

Bind off as to purl.

Sew other shoulder seam; sew trim seam.

ARMHOLE TRIM:
Note: *Stitches may need to be added or subtracted to ensure that trim lies flat.*

Row 1 (right side)**:** Hold top with right side facing; pick up 132 (136, 140) sts evenly spaced along straight armhole edge between underarm bind-offs.

Row 2: * K2 tog; P2 tog; rep from * across: 66 (68, 70) sts.

Row 3: Inc (knit in front and back of next st) in each st.

Row 4: * P2 tog; K2 tog; rep from * across.

Bind off as to purl.

Repeat for other armhole trim.

Sew sides of trim to bound-off armhole edge, then sew side seams.

LION'S MANE EVENING TOP

Designed by Sandy Scoville

Note: *Instructions are written for size Small; changes for sizes Medium and Large are in parentheses.*

Size:	Small	Medium	Large
Body Chest Measurements:	30"–32"	32"–34"	34"–36"
Finished Chest Measurement:	34"	36"	38"

Time to make: About 21 hours

MATERIALS:

Bulky Fur-type yarn, 425 (465, 505) yds; variegated gold

Note: *Photographed model made with Crystal Palace Splash®, #7183 Lioness.*

Size 9 (5.5 mm) knitting needles, or size required for gauge

Stitch holder

4 small safety pins

GAUGE:

17 sts = 4" in Reverse Stockinette Stitch

Instructions:

FRONT:

Cast on 63 (67, 71) sts.

Row 1 (right side)**:** Purl.

Row 2: Knit.

Rep Rows 1 and 2 until piece measures about 12" (12½", 13"), ending by working a right-side row.

Mark each side of last row with contrasting yarn or safety pin for underarms.

Dividing Row (wrong side)**:**

For Right Front Shoulder, inc (knit in front and back of next st); K30 (32, 34); slip these sts onto stitch holder;

For Center Front, sl 1, K1, PSSO;

For Left Front Shoulder, knit to last st; inc: 32 (34, 36) sts on each shoulder.

LEFT FRONT SHOULDER AND NECKLINE Shaping:

Row 1 (right side)**:** P30 (32, 34), P2 tog: 31 (33, 35) sts.

Row 2: Sl 1, K1, PSSO; knit to last st; inc.

Row 3: Purl to last 2 sts; P2 tog: 30 (32, 34) sts.

Rows 4 through 9: Rep Rows 2 and 3 three times: 27 (29, 31) sts.

Row 10: Sl 1, K1, PSSO; knit across: 26 (28, 30) sts.

Row 11: Purl to last 2 sts; P2 tog: 25 (27, 29) sts.

Rows 12 and 13: Rep Rows 2 and 3: 24 (26, 28) sts.

Rows 14 through 17: Rep Rows 10 through 13: 21 (23, 25) sts.

71

continued on page 72

LION'S MANE EVENING TOP
continued

Rows 18 through 21: Rep Rows 10 and 11 twice: 17 (19, 21) sts.

Row 22: Knit.

Row 23: Purl.

Rep Rows 22 and 23 until left front shoulder measures 7″ (7 ½″, 7 ½″) from marked row, ending with a right-side row.

Bind off.

RIGHT FRONT SHOULDER AND NECKLINE SHAPING:
Slip sts from holder onto needle. Hold in left hand with right side facing.

Row 1 (right side)**:** Sl 1, P1, PSSO; P30 (32, 34): 31 (33, 35) sts.

Row 2: Inc; knit to last 2 sts; K2 tog.

Row 3: Sl 1, P1, PSSO; purl across: 30 (32, 34) sts.

Rows 4 through 9: Rep Rows 2 and 3, three times: 27 (29, 31) sts.

Row 10: Knit to last 2 sts; K2 tog: 26 (28, 30) sts.

Row 11: Sl 1, P1, PSSO; purl across: 25 (27, 29) sts.

Rows 12 and 13: Rep Rows 2 and 3: 24 (26, 28) sts.

Rows 14 through 17: Rep Rows 10 through 13: 21 (23, 25) sts.

Rows 18 through 21: Rep Rows 10 and 11, twice: 17 (19, 21) sts.

Row 22: Knit.

Row 23: Purl.

Rep Rows 22 and 23 until right front shoulder measures same as left front shoulder.

Bind off. Do not remove markers.

BACK
Work same as for front until piece measures same as front to marked row. Mark row as for front.

Row 1 (right side)**:** Purl.

Row 2: Inc; knit to last st; inc: 65 (69, 73) sts.

Rows 3 through 8: Rep Rows 1 and 2 three times: 71 (75, 79) sts.

Row 9: Purl.

Row 10 (dividing row)**: For Left Back Shoulder,** inc; K24 (26, 28), K2 tog; slip these sts onto stitch holder.

For Center Back Neckline, bind off next 17 (17, 17) sts.

For Right Back Shoulder, slip st on right-hand needle to left-hand needle; K2 tog tbl; K24 (26, 28); inc: 27 (29, 31) sts on each side.

RIGHT BACK NECKLINE SHAPING:
Row 1 (right side)**:** P25 (26, 28); P2 tog: 26 (28, 30) sts.

Row 2: Sl 1, K1, PSSO; knit across: 25 (27, 29) sts.

Row 3: P23 (25, 27); P2 tog: 24 (26, 28) sts.

Row 4: Sl 1, K1, PSSO; knit to last st; inc.

Rows 5 through 8: Rep Rows 1 through 4: 21 (23, 25) sts.

Row 1: P2 tog tbl; P25 (27, 29): 26 (28, 30) sts.

Row 2: Knit to last 2 sts; K2 tog: 25 (27, 29) sts.

Row 3: P2 tog tbl; purl across: 24 (26, 28) sts.

Row 4: Inc; knit to last 2 sts; K2 tog.

Rows 5 through 8: Rep Rows 1 through 4: 21 (23, 25) sts.

Row 9: Rep Row 3: 20 (22, 24) sts

Rows 10 and 11: Rep Rows 2 and 3. At end of Row 11: 18 (20, 22) sts.

Row 12: Rep Row 2: 17 (19, 21) sts

Row 13: Purl.

Row 14: Knit.

Row 15: Purl.

Rep Rows 14 and 15 until Left Back Shoulder measures same as Front Back Shoulder. Bind off. Do not remove markers.

Sew shoulder seams. Sew side seams from cast-on edges to markers. Remove markers. Weave in ends.

Row 9: Rep Row 3: 20 (22, 24) sts.

Rows 10 and 11: Rep Rows 2 and 3: 18 (20, 22) sts.

Row 12: Rep Row 2: 17 (19, 21) sts.

Row 13: Purl.

Row 14: Knit.

Row 15: Purl.

Rep Rows 14 and 15 until Right Back measures same as Left Front. Bind off. Do not remove markers.

LEFT BACK NECKLINE SHAPING:
Slip sts on holder onto left needle and hold with right side facing.

BOUCLÉ TOP

Designed by Sandy Scoville

Note: *Instructions are written for size Small; changes for sizes Medium and Large are in parentheses.*

Size:	Small	Medium	Large
Body Chest Measurements:	30"–32"	34"–36"	38"–40"
Finished Chest Measurement:	32"	36"	40"

Time to knit: About 18 hours

MATERIALS:

Bulky weight boucle yarn, 25 (27, 29) oz, variegated; worsted weight yarn, 1 oz, purple (all sizes)

Note: *Photographed model made with Lion Brand Lion Bouclé, Color #205 Sorbet, and Bernat® So Soft®, Color #75330, Ultra Violet*

Size 10 ½ (6.5 mm) knitting needles, or size required for gauge

2 large stitch holders

GAUGE:

With bulky weight yarn, 5 sts = 2" in Stockinette Stitch (knit one row, purl one row)

Instructions:

BACK:

With variegated yarn, cast on 46 (48, 50) sts.

Rows 1 through 3: Knit.

Row 4 (wrong side): Purl.

Row 5 (right side): Knit.

Row 6: Purl.

Rows 7 through 10: Rep Rows 5 and 6.

Change to purple, but do not cut variegated; carry along side edge.

Rows 11 through 12: Knit.

Row 13: Purl.

Row 14: Knit. Cut purple.

With variegated, continue in st st until piece measures 13" (13½" 14"), ending by working a wrong-side row.

ARMHOLE SHAPING:

Row 1 (right side): Bind off 3 sts; knit across.

Row 2: Bind off 3 sts; purl across: 40 (42, 44) sts.

Continue in st st until armhole measures 7"(7½", 8"), ending by working a wrong-side row.

RIGHT BACK SHOULDER AND NECKLINE SHAPING:

Row 1 (right side): K8, K2 tog; slip rem sts onto stitch holder: 9 sts on needle.

Row 2: Purl.

Row 3: K7, K2 tog: 8 sts.

Row 4: Purl.

Bind off.

LEFT BACK SHOULDER AND NECKLINE SHAPING:

Slip 10 sts from stitch holder onto left-hand needle, leaving rem sts on holder for neckline.

Row 1 (right side): K2 tog tbl; K8: 9 sts.

Row 2: Purl.

Row 3: K2 tog tbl; K7: 8 sts.

Row 4: Purl.

Bind off.

FRONT:

Work same as back through Row 2 of armhole shaping: 40 (42, 44) sts.

Continue in stock st until piece measures about 4" (4½", 5").

LEFT FRONT SHOULDER AND NECKLINE SHAPING:

Row 1 (right side): K13, K2 tog: 14 sts. Slip rem sts onto stitch holder.

Row 2: Purl.

Rows 3: Knit to last 2 sts, K2 tog.

Row 4: Purl.

Rows 5 through 14: Rep Rows 3 and 4. At end of Row 14: 8 sts.

Bind off.

continued on page 76

BOUCLÉ TOP
continued

RIGHT FRONT SHOULDER AND NECKLINE SHAPING:

Slip 15 sts at arm edge from stitch holder to left-hand needle, leaving rem sts on holder for front neckline.

Row 1 (right side): K2 tog tbl; knit rem sts: 14 sts.

Row 2: Purl.

Rows 3 through 14: Rep Rows 1 and 2. At end of Row 14: 8 sts.

Bind off.

Sew left shoulder seam.

NECKLINE SHAPING:

Row 1 (right side): Beginning at right back shoulder and working around neckline, with variegated, pick up 4 sts to back stitch holder; knit 20 (22, 24) sts from stitch holder; pick up 4 sts to shoulder seam, pick up 15 sts to front stitch holder; knit 10 (12, 14) sts from stitch holder, pick up 15 sts along shoulder shaping: 68 (72, 76) sts.

Drop variegated to wrong side of work. Join purple in first stitch on Row 1.

Row 2 (right side): With purple, knit.

Row 3: Knit.

Row 4: Purl. Cut purple.

Row 5 (wrong side): With variegated, purl.

Row 6 (right side): Purl.

Row 7: Knit.

Bind off as to purl.

Sew shoulder and neckline seam.

SLEEVE (make 2)

With variegated, cast on 33 (37, 37) sts.

Row 1 (right side): Knit.

Row 2: Knit.

Row 3: K2 tog; * K5, K2 tog; rep from * 3 (4, 4) times more; K3 (0, 0): 28 (31, 31) sts.

Row 4: Purl.

Row 5: * K5, K2 tog; rep from * 2 (3, 3) times more; K7 (3, 3): 25 (27, 27) sts.

Row 6: Purl.

Row 7: K2 tog; knit to last 2 sts; K2 tog: 23 (25, 25) sts.

Row 8: Purl.

Row 9: Knit.

Row 10: Purl.

Change to purple; carry variegated along side edge.

Row 11: With purple, knit.

Row 12: Knit.

Row 13: Purl.

Row 14: Knit. Cut purple.

Row 15: With variegated, knit.

Row 16: Purl.

Row 17: Inc (knit in front and back of next st); knit to last st; inc: 25 (27, 27) sts.

Row 18: Purl.

Row 19: Knit.

Row 20: Purl.

Rows 21 and 22: Rep Rows 19 and 20.

Rep Rows 17 through 22 until there are 41 (43, 47) sts on needle.

Continue in st st (without inc) until sleeve measures 21" (21", 22") from cast-on row, ending by working a wrong-side row.
Bind off.

Repeat for other sleeve.

Sew sleeves to armhole edges. Sew underarm and side seams.

FORECAST FOR FALL VEST

Designed by Sandy Scoville

Note: *Instructions are written for size Small; changes for sizes Medium and Large are in parentheses.*

Size:	Small	Medium	Large
Body Chest Measurements:	28″–30″	32″–34″	36″–38″
Finished Chest Measurement:	34″	36″	38″

Time to make: About 17 hours

MATERIALS:

Light worsted weight yarn, 17 (18, 19) oz, dark red

Bulky weight "fur" type yarn, 125 yds, red/purple variegated

Note: *Photographed model made with TLC® Amoré™, Color #3782 Garnet, and Crystal Palace Splash®, Color #7234 Carnival.*

14″ straight knitting needles, Size 9 (5.5 mm) or size required for gauge

Stitch holder

Size H (5 mm) crochet hook

GAUGE:

7 sts = 2″ in Stockinette Stitch (knit one row, purl one row)

Instructions:

Note: *Vest is made with 2 strands of yarn held together.*

Back: Starting at lower edge with 2 strands of dark red held tog, cast on 60 (63, 66) sts.

Row 1 (right side): Purl.

Row 2: Purl.

Row 3: Knit.

Row 4: Purl.

Rep Rows 3 and 4 until piece measures 11″ (11½″, 12″) from cast-on edge, ending by

working a wrong-side row.

ARMHOLE SHAPING:

Row 1 (right side): Bind off 5 sts; knit across.

Row 2: Bind off 5 sts; purl across: 50 (53, 56) sts.

Row 3: Sl 1 as to knit, K1, PSSO; knit to last 2 sts; K2 tog: 48 (51, 54) sts.

Row 4: Purl.

Row 5: Rep Row 3. At end of row: 46 (49, 52) sts.

Continue in St St until armhole measures 6″ (6″, 6½″), ending by working a wrong-side row.

NECKLINE SHAPING:

Row 1 (right side): For right back shoulder, K 16 (17, 18), slip just knit stitches onto stitch holder; bind off next 14 (15, 16) sts; for left back shoulder, K16 (17, 18).

Row 2: Purl.

LEFT BACK SHOULDER SHAPING:

Row 1 (right side): Sl 1 as to knit, K1, PSSO; knit across: 15 (16, 17) sts.

Row 2: Purl.

Rows 3 through 4: Rep Rows 1 and 2.

Row 5: Rep Row 1. At end of Row 5: 13 (14, 15) sts.

Bind off.

RIGHT BACK SHOULDER SHAPING:

Hold back with wrong side facing; slip stitches from holder onto needle; with 2 strands of dark red held together, purl across.

Row 1 (right side): Knit to last 2 sts; K2 tog: 15 (16, 17) sts.

Row 2: Purl

Rows 3 through 4: Rep Rows 1 and 2. At end of Row 4: 14 (15, 16) sts.

Row 5: Rep Row 1. At end of row: 13 (14, 15) sts.

Bind off.

RIGHT FRONT:

With 2 strands of dark red held tog, cast on 29 (30, 31) sts.

Rows 1 (right side): Purl.

Row 2: Purl.

Row 3: Knit.

Row 4: Purl.

Rep Rows 3 and 4 until piece measures same as back to underarm shaping.

continued on page 78

FORECAST FOR FALL VEST
continued

NECKLINE AND UNDERARM SHAPING:
Row 1 (right side)**:** Starting at neck edge, sl 1 as to knit, K1, PSSO; knit to last 2 sts; K2 tog: 27 (28, 29) sts.

Row 2: Purl to last 2 sts; P2 tog: 26 (27, 28) sts.

Rows 3 through 4: Rep Rows 1 and 2. At end of Row 4: 23 (24, 25) sts.

Row 5: Sl 1 as to knit, K1, PSSO; knit across: 22 (23, 24) sts.

Row 6: Purl to last 2 sts; P2 tog: 21 (22, 23) sts.

Rows 7 through 14: Rep Rows 5 and 6 four times more. At end of Row 14: 13 (14, 15) sts.

Work in st st without dec until right front measures same as back.

Bind off.

LEFT FRONT:
With 2 strands of dark red held tog, cast on 29 (30, 31) sts.

Row 1 (right side)**:** Purl.

Row 2: Purl.

Row 3: Knit.

Row 4: Purl.

Rep Rows 3 and 4 until piece measures same as back to underarm shaping.

UNDERARM AND NECKLINE SHAPING:
Row 1 (right side)**:** Sl 1, K1, PSSO; knit to last 2 sts; K2 tog: 27 (28, 29) sts.

Row 2: P2 tog tbl; purl across: 26 (27, 28) sts.

Rows 3 through 4: Rep Rows 1 and 2. At end of Row 6: 23 (24, 25) sts.

Row 5: Knit to last 2 sts; K2 tog: 22 (23, 24) sts.

Row 6: P2 tog tbl; purl across: 21 (22, 23) sts.

Rows 7 through 14: Rep Rows 5 and 6.

At end of Row 14: 13 (14, 15) sts.

Work in St St without dec until front measures same as back.

Bind off.

Sew shoulder seams.

CENTER FRONT EDGING:
Hold vest with right side facing and center edge of right front at top; join 2 strands of dark red in side of first row.

Row 1 (right side)**:** Working around center front and neckline edge, pick up and knit 2 sts for every 3 rows along right front and shoulder to center back, 1 st in each bound-off st across center back, and 2 sts for every 3 rows along left front edge.

Row 2: Knit.

Row 3: Purl.

Bind off.

ARMHOLE TRIM:
Hold vest with right side facing and one armhole edge at top.

Row 1 (right side)**:** With one strand of variegated, pick up and knit 1 in each bound-off st at underarm and in side of each row along armhole edge.

Row 2: Knit.

Row 3: Purl.

Rows 4 and 5: Rep Rows 2 and 3.

Bind off.

Work other underarm trim in same manner.

Sew trim and side seams.

NECKLINE TRIM:
Hold vest with right side facing and center right front edge at top; join one strand of variegated in first decrease row of neckline

shaping.

Row 1 (right side)**:** Pick up and knit one st in each st around neck edge.

Row 2: K2 tog; knit to last 2 sts; K2 tog.

Row 3: P2 tog; purl to last 2 sts; P2 tog.

Rows 4 through 7: Rep Rows 2 and 3.

Bind off.

FORECAST FOR FALL HAT

Designed by Sandy Scoville

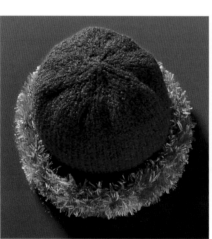

Time to make: About 7 hours

SIZE:

21" circumference

MATERIALS:

Light worsted weight yarn, 2 oz, dark red
Bulky weight "fur" type yarn, 125 yds,
  red/purple variegated

Note: *Photographed model made with
TLC® Amoré™ , Color #3782 Garnet,
and Crystal Palace Splash, Color
#7234 Carnival.*

14" straight knitting needles Size 10
  (6 mm), or size required for gauge
Size 16 tapestry needle

GAUGE:

6 sts = 2" in Stockinette Stitch (knit one
row, purl one row)

Instructions:

CUFF:

Starting at lower edge with variegated, cast
on 63 sts.

Row 1 (right side)**:** Purl.

Row 2: Knit.

Rep Rows 1 and 2 until cuff measures
about 3 ½", ending by working a wrong-
side row. Cut variegated yarn.

Note: *Remainder of hat is worked with 2
strands of dark red held together.*

BODY:

Row 1 (wrong side)**:** With 2 strands of dark
red held tog, knit.

Row 2 (right side)**:** Knit.

Row 3: Purl.

Rep Rows 2 and 3 until crown measures 5″ from cuff, ending by working a wrong-side row.

CROWN:

Row 1 (right side)**:** * K1, K2 tog; rep from * across: 42 sts.

Row 2: Purl.

Row 3: * K2 tog; K1; rep from * across: 28 sts.

Row 4: Purl.

Row 5: K1; * K2 tog; K1; rep from * across: 19 sts.

Row 6: Purl.

Row 7: Rep Row 5. At end of Row 7: 13 sts.

Row 8: Purl.

Row 9: K1; (K2 tog) 6 times: 7 sts.

Cut yarn, leaving a 20″ end for sewing.

Thread yarn into tapestry needle; weave yarn through rem 7 sts, removing from needle; pull to close.

Carefully matching rows, sew seam to cuff. With variegated, sew cuff seam.

Weave in ends..

Fold cuff up.

RIBBON FRINGE SCARF

Designed by Carol Wilson Mansfield

Time to make: 10 hours including fringe

SIZE:

8" x 72"

MATERIALS:

12 oz worsted weight yarn, cream

Note: *Photographed model made with*
Red Heart® Plush™ Color #9103, Cream.

Assorted narrow ribbons, cream or white,
about 40 yds

Size 8 (5 mm) knitting needles or size
required for gauge.

GAUGE:

9 sts = 2"

Instructions

Cast on 35 sts.

Knit two rows for foundation.

PATTERN ROWS

Row 1: (K 5, P 5) across row.

Row 2: (P 5, K 5) across row.

Rows 3 through 6: Rep Rows 1 and 2 twice.

Row 7: (P 5, K 5) across row.

Row 8: (K 5, P 5) across row.

Rows 9 through 12: Rep Rows 7 and 8 twice.

Rep Rows 1 through 12 in sequence until piece measures about 72" long, ending by working Rows 1 through 6. Purl two rows, bind off.

FRINGE:

Cut ribbons and remaining yarn into 14" lengths. For each knot, combine 2 strands of yarn with two or 3 strands of ribbon, using a variety of ribbons. Following fringe instructions on page 123, make 8 knots of fringe between the first two rows at each short end, knotting between intersections of K and P sts, and at each outside edge.

POCKET SHAWL

Designed by Sandy Scoville

Time to make: About 21 hours

SIZE:
About 12" x 64"

MATERIALS:
Bulky weight yarn, 10 oz, coral
Note: *Photographed model made
with Lion Brand® Homespun,
Color #370 Coral Gables.*
Size 9 (5.5 mm) knitting needles,
or size required for gauge
Size 16 tapestry needle
Cable needle

GAUGE:

3 sts = 1" in Stockinette Stitch (knit one row, purl one row)

PATTERN STITCH:

Cable Front (CF): Slip 3 sts onto cable needle and hold in front; K3, K3 from cable needle: CF made.

Instructions:

Cast on 39 sts.

Row 1 (right side): Purl.

Row 2: Knit.

Row 3 (right side): K3; * P1, K3; rep from * across.

Row 4: P3; * K1, P3; rep from * across.

Rep Rows 1 and 2 until shawl measures about 64", ending by working a wrong side row.

Next Row: Purl.

Bind off.

Pockets (make 2): Cast on 39 sts.

Row 1 (right side): Purl.

Row 2: Knit.

Row 3: (K6, P2) twice; K7, (P2, K6) twice.

Row 4: (P6, K2) twice; P7, (K2, P6) twice.

Rows 5 and 6: Rep Rows 3 and 4.

Row 7: K6, P2, CF (see Pattern Stitch); P2, K7, P2, CF; P2, K6.

Row 8: Rep Row 4.

Rows 9 and 10: Rep Rows 3 and 4.

Rows 11 through 42: Rep Rows 3 through 10 four times.

Row 43: Purl.

Bind off.

FINISHING:

Place one pocket on one end of shawl with right sides of both pieces facing you. Pocket will be narrower than shawl; center pocket with lower edge at lower edge of shawl; do not stretch pocket. With tapestry needle and yarn, carefully sew together along sides and lower edge of pocket. Tack top edge of pocket to shawl about 1½" from each side edge.

Sew other pocket at opposite end of shawl.

YUMMY THROW

Designed by Sandy Scoville

Time to make: About 19 hours

SIZE:
About 48" x 52"

MATERIALS:
Bulky weight chenille yarn, 675 yds brown
Note: *Photographed model made with Lion Brand Chenille Thick & Quick®, Color #227 Desert Print.*
29" circular knitting needle, Size 11, or size required for gauge

GAUGE:
2 sts = 1" in Stockinette Stitch (knit one row, purl one row)

Instructions:
Note: *Throw is reversible.*

Loosely cast on 92 sts; do not join. Work back and forth in rows.

LOWER EDGING:
Row 1: Purl.

Row 2: Knit.

BODY:

Row 1: K11; * P10, K10; rep from * 3 times more; K1.

Row 2: K1, P10; * K10, P10; rep from * 3 times more; K1.

Rows 3 through 20: Rep Rows 1 and 2.

Row 21: K1, P10; * K10, P10; rep from * 3 times more; K1.

Row 22: K11; * P10, K10; rep from * 3 times more; K1.

Rows 23 through 40: Rep Rows 21 and 22.

Rep Rows 1 through 40 four times more.

TOP EDGING:

Row 1: Purl.

Row 2: Knit.

Bind off as to knit.

87

WEARIN' OF THE GREEN SCARF

Designed by Carol Wilson Mansfield

Time to make: About 14 hours

SIZE:
9" x 73"

MATERIALS:
Worsted weight yarn, 4 ozs green
Note: *Photographed model made
with Red Heart® Hokey Pokey™,
Color #7110 (Spearmint).*
Size 10 (6 mm) knitting needles or size
required for gauge
60 small round beads, multicolor
beading needle

GAUGE:
9 sts = 2"

Instructions:
Cast on 38 sts and knit two rows for foundation.

Row 1: K8; * K2 tog, YO, K1, YO; sl 1, K1, PSSO*; K12; rep from * to * once; K8.

Row 2 (and all even rows)**:** K2, working each YO as a st, purl to last 2 sts, K2.

Row 3: K7; * K2 tog, YO, K3, YO; sl 1, K1, PSSO*; K10; rep from * to * once, K7.

Row 5: K6; * K2 tog, YO, K5, YO; sl 1, K1, PSSO*; K8, rep from * to * once, K6.

Row 7: K5; * K2 tog, YO, K7, YO; sl 1, K1, PSSO*; K6, rep from * to * once, K5.

Row 9: K4; * K2 tog, YO, K9, YO; sl 1, K1, PSSO* ; K4, rep from * to *, K4.

Row 11: K3; * K2 tog, YO, K11, YO; sl 1, K1, PSSO*; K2, rep from * to *, K3.

Row 13: Rep Row 9.

Row 15: Rep Row 7.

Row 17: Rep Row 5.

Row 19: Rep Row 3.

Row 20: Rep Row 2.

Rep Rows 1 through 20 until scarf measures about 72" long, ending by working a Row 2.

Knit two rows, then bind off loosely. Weave in ends.

FRINGE:
Following Fringe instructions on page 123, cut two 12" long strands of yarn for each knot. Thread each length into beading needle, add beads as desired, alternating placement and knotting yarn below each bead. Tie knots at each outer edge and every third st across each short end.

WEARIN' OF THE GREEN HAT

Designed by Carol Wilson Mansfield

Time to make: About 6 hours

SIZE:

Fits up to 23" head

MATERIALS:

Worsted weight yarn, 4 ozs green

Note: *Photographed model made with Red Heart® Hokey Pokey™, Color # 7110 Spearmint.*

Size 10 (6 mm) straight knitting needles, or size required for gauge

Size 8 (5 mm) straight knitting needles

Size 8 (5 mm) double point knitting needles

Approximately 25 small round beads, multicolor

Beading needle

GAUGE:

With size 10 needles, 9 sts = 2"

Instructions:

BODY:

Starting at cuff with size 10 needles, cast on 78 sts.

Rows 1 through 7: Knit.

Change to smaller needles.

Rows 8, 10 & 12: Knit.

Rows 9, 11 & 13: Purl.

Change to larger needles and work pattern as follows:

Rows 1 through 40: Following instructions for Wearin' of the Green Scarf on page 88, work Rows 1 through 20 twice.

BODY:

Eyelet Pattern:

Row 1: K4,* K3, K2 tog, YO; rep from * across, ending K4.

Row 2: K2, working each YO as a stitch, P to last 2 sts, K2.

Row 3: Knit.

Row 4: * K2, P 2, rep from * across, ending K2.

Rep Rows 3 and 4 once. Bind off.

FINISHING:

Fold hat in half lengthwise, right sides facing, and sew seam along long side. Weave in ends.

Turn to right side and turn up cuff.

TOP TRIM:

Cord:

On one double point needle, cast on 4 sts, leaving a 6" yarn end.

* K4; hold needle with sts in left hand again, slide sts to opposite end of needle, K4, pulling yarn across back of sts; rep from * until cord measures about 18" long; bind off, leaving a 6" yarn end. Weave cord through eyelets at top of hat.

Tassel (make 2):

Following tassel instructions on page 124, cut 12 strands 9" long. Following fringe instructions for scarf on page 123 add beads to each strand. With long yarn ends left on cord, sew tassels to each end of cord. Draw up cord and tie.

VERY SUITABLE SWEATER

Designed by Sandy Scoville

Note: *Instructions are written for size Small; changes for sizes Medium and Large are in parentheses.*

Size:	Small	Medium	Large
Body Chest Measurements:	32"–34"	36"–38"	40"–42"
Finished Chest Measurement:	34"	38"	42"

Time to make: About 19 hours

MATERIALS:

Light worsted weight yarn, 13 (14, 15) oz, blue

Note: Photographed model made with Red Heart® Plush™, Color #9823 French Blue.

14" straight knitting needles, Size 5 (3.75 mm) or size required for gauge

GAUGE:

18 sts = 4" in Stockinette Stitch (knit one row, purl one row)

Instructions:

BACK:

Ribbing:

Cast on 81 (89, 97) sts.

Row 1 (right side)**:** K1; * P1, K1; rep from * across.

Row 2: P1; * K1, P1; rep from * across.

Rows 3 through 12: Rep Rows 1 and 2.

Body:

Size Small Only:

Row 1 (right side)**:** K2 * K5, P1, K1, P1, K7, P1, K1, P1; rep from * 3 times more; K7.

Row 2: P7; * K1, P1, K1, P7, K1, P1, K1, P5; rep from * 3 times more; P2.

Continue with All Sizes below.

Sizes Medium and Large Only:

Row 1 (right side)**:** K3 (7); P1, K1, P1, * K5, P1, K1, P1, K7, P1, K1, P1; rep from * 3 times more; K5, P1, K1, P1; ending by working K3 (7).

Row 2: P3 (7); K1, P1, K1, P5, * K1, P1, K1, P7, K1, P1, K1, P5; rep from * 3 times more; K1, P1, K1; ending by working P3 (7).

All Sizes:

Continue in pattern until body measures about 13" from beg, ending on a wrong side row.

ARMHOLE AND SHOULDER SHAPING:

Row 1 (right side)**:** Bind off 4 (4, 6) sts; work in patt across.

Row 2: Bind off 4 (4, 6) sts; work in patt across: 73 (81, 85) sts.

Continue in patt until armhole measures about 6½" (7", 7"), ending on a wrong side row.

NECKLINE SHAPING:

Row 1 (right side)**:** Work 22 (26, 26) sts in patt; join 2nd strand of yarn, bind off 29 (29, 33) sts, work in patt across.

Row 2: Work in patt across both shoulders.

Row 3: On right shoulder, work in patt to last 2 sts, K2 tog; on left shoulder, slip 1 as to knit, K1, PSSO, work in patt across: 21 (25, 25) sts on each shoulder.

Rows 4 through 11: Rep Rows 2 and 3. At end of Row 11: 17 (21, 21) sts on each shoulder.

Bind off in patt.

FRONT:

Work as for back until armhole measures 5½" (6, 6) inches, ending by working a wrong side row.

NECKLINE SHAPING:

Row 1 (right side)**:** Work 26 (30, 30) sts in patt; join 2nd strand of yarn, bind off 21 (21, 25) sts, work in patt across.

Row 2: Work in patt across.

Row 3: On left shoulder, work in patt to last 2 sts, K2 tog; on right shoulder, sl 1 as to knit, K1, PSSO, work in patt across: 25 (29, 29) sts on each shoulder.

Rows 4 through 19: Rep Rows 2 and 3. At end of Row 19: 17 (21, 21) sts on each shoulder.

Work even in patt until front measures same as back.

Bind off.

Sew right shoulder seam.

COLLAR:

Row 1 (right side)**:** Starting at left shoulder, pick up and knit 99 (99, 103) sts around neckline.

Row 2: K1, * P1, K1, rep from * across.

Row 3: P1, * K1, P1, rep from * across.

Rep Rows 2 and 3 until collar measures about 8". Bind off in ribbing.

Sew right shoulder seam, leaving collar open. Fold open side of collar forward.

Weave in ends.

LET THE WINDS BLOW

Time to make: About 8 hours

SIZE:
6" x 72"

MATERIALS:
Worsted weight yarn, 7 oz wine
Note: *Photographed model made with*
   Red Heart® Plush™ #9782 Wine.
Size 8 (5 mm) knitting needles, or size
   required for gauge

GAUGE
14 sts = 3" in K1, P1 ribbing.

Instructions:

Cast on 28 sts.

Row 1: * K 1, P 1, rep from * across row.

Row 2 and all following rows: Rep
Row 1.

Work until scarf measures 72". Bind off.

FRINGE:
Follow Single Knot Fringe on page 123.
Cut strands 14" long. Use three strands for
each knot. Tie knot in every other stitch
across each end.

BRIGHT & BEAUTIFUL SCARF

Designed by Sandy Scoville

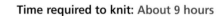

Time required to knit: About 9 hours

SIZE:
About 7" x 70"

MATERIALS:
Worsted weight nylon "eyelash" yarn,
    5 ¼ oz variegated red/violet
*Note: Photographed model made
    with Patons® Cha Cha, Color #2003
    Be Bop.*
Size 10 (6 mm) knitting needles

GAUGE:
4 sts = 1" in Stockinette Stitch (knit one
row, purl one row)

Instructions:

Note: Scarf is reversible.

Cast on 30 sts.

Row 1: Knit.

Row 2: Purl.

Rep Rows 1 and 2 until scarf measures
about 70".

Bind off.

BRIGHT & BEAUTIFUL HAT

Designed by Sandy Scoville

Time to make: About 5 hours

SIZE:

Fits 19" to 21" head

MATERIALS:

Worsted weight nylon "fur" or "eyelash" yarn, 1¾ oz variegated red/violet

Note: *Photographed model was made with Patons® Cha Cha, Color #2003 Be Bop.*

Size 8 (5 mm) knitting needles

Size 16 tapestry needle

GAUGE:

9 sts = 2" in Stockinette Stitch (knit one row, purl one row)

Note: *Yarn stretches. Check gauge carefully.*

Instructions:

Cast on 86 sts.

CUFF:

Row 1 (right side)**:** * K1, P1; rep from * across.

Rep Row 1 until Cuff measures about 4".

Turning Row: Knit.

BODY:

Row 1 (right side)**:** Knit.

Row 2: Purl.

Rep Rows 1 and 2 until hat measures 10", ending by working a wrong-side row.

CROWN:

Row 1 (right side)**:** K2 tog; * K1, K2 tog; rep from * across: 57 sts.

Row 2: Purl.

Row 3: * K2 tog; K1; rep from * across: 38 sts.

Row 4: Purl.

Row 5: Rep Row 1. At end of row: 25 sts.

Row 6: Purl.

Row 7: K1, (K2 tog) 12 times: 13 sts.

Row 8: Purl.

Row 9: (K2 tog) 6 times; K1: 7 sts.

Row 10: Purl.

Row 11: K1, (K2 tog) 3 times: 4 sts.

Cut yarn, leaving a 24" end for sewing.

Insert yarn end into tapestry needle and draw through sts on needle twice; remove sts from needle and draw tight.

Carefully matching rows, sew back seam. Fold cuff up at turning row.

DANCING DAYS

Time to Make: 12 hours 45 minutes

SIZE:

About 46" x 47" (or desired length)

MATERIALS:

Worsted weight yarn, 12 ozs.

Note: *Photographed model made with Bernat® Antique Christmas, Color #94430 Golden Burgundy.*

36" circular knitting needle, Size 10 ½ (6.5 mm), or size required for gauge

GAUGE:

4 sts = 1" in Garter Stitch (knit each row)

Instructions:

Note: Circular needle is used to accommodate the large number of stitches. Do not join; work back and forth in rows.

Cast on 4 sts.

Row 1: Knit, increasing 1 st at the beg and end of the row by knitting into the front and back of the first and last stitch.

Rows 2 and 3: Repeat row 1.

Row 4: * K1, YO 3 times; rep from * to last st, K1.

Row 5: * K1, drop all YO's from needle; rep from * to last st, K1. Gently tug on dropped sts so that they lie flat.

Row 6: Knit, pulling on dropped sts across row.

Rep these 6 rows until you have repeated the pattern 27 times more (or until shawl is desired length).

Bind off loosely.

Make 5 1/2″ fringe following the instructions for making fringes given on page 123.

Attach fringe along both edges of Row 1 along sides of the shawl and place a fringe at the bottom point.

97

VESTED INTEREST

Note: Instructions are written for size 38; changes for sizes 40", 42" and 44" are in parentheses.

Size:	Small	Medium	Large	Extra Large
Body Bust Measurements:	38"	40"	42"	44"
Finished Garment Measurement:	42"	44"	46"	48"

Time to make: About 19 1/2 hours

MATERIALS:

Bulky weight yarn: 18 (18-20-22) oz

Note: Photographed model made with Lion Brand Homespun®, Color #335 Prairie.

36" circular knitting needles size 10 (6 mm), or size required for gauge.

2 large stitch holders

GAUGE:

5 sts = 2" in garter stitch (knit every row).

Note: Circular needle is used to accommodate large number of stitches. Do not join. Work back and forth in rows.

Instructions:

BACK:

Cast on 51 (53, 55, 57) sts.

Work in garter stitch until piece measures 17 (17, 18,18) inches. Put all sts on a stitch holder and cut yarn.

RIGHT FRONT:

Cast on 25 (26, 27, 28) sts. Work in garter stitch until piece measures same as back. Put all sts on a stitch holder and cut yarn.

LEFT FRONT:

Work same as right front, but at end, do not cut yarn; knit one more row on left front, then join pieces as follows:

BODY:

Work across all stitches from back stitch holder, then work all stitches from right front stitch holder: 101 (105, 109,113) sts. Work in garter stitch until piece measures 30 (30", 31", 32") from cast-on edge.

DIVIDE FOR ARMHOLES:

Knit across first 25 (26, 27, 28) sts, mark this row; put rem st on a holder

Work in garter st on these 25 (26, 27, 28) sts until piece measures 9" (9 1/2", 10", 10 1/2") from marked row. Bind off.

Knit 51 (53, 55, 57) sts from st holder, mark this row. Work until piece measures 9" (9½", 10", 10") from marked row. Bind off.

Knit last (25, 26, 27, 29) sts from st holder, mark this row. Work until piece measures 9" (9½", 10", 10½") from st holder, mark this row. Work until piece measures 9" (9½", 10", 10½") from marked row. Bind off.

FINISHING:
Sew right and left shoulder seams, leaving center st.

Weave in ends.

Time to make: About 1 hour

SIZE:
Approx 10" x 42"

MATERIALS:
"Eyelash" type yarn, 1½ oz in color of
 your choice
Size 13 (9 mm) straight knitting needles

GAUGE:
About 3 st = 1"

Instructions
Cast on 30 sts loosely, leaving a 12" tail
at beg.

Row 1: Knit.

Rep Row 1 until scarf measures about 42"
long (or desired length).

Bind off loosely, leaving a 12" tail.

Weave in ends along each edge.

BOUDOIR AFGHAN

Time to make: 20 hours (including fringe)

SIZE:

40" x 51" before fringing

MATERIALS:

Brushed mohair-type bulky yarn 23 oz

Note: *Photographed model made with Lion Brand Jiffy®, Midnight Blues #360.*

36" circular needle, Size 11 (8 mm), or size required for gauge

10 stitch markers

GAUGE:

10 sts = 3 in garter st (knit every row)

Notes: Circular needles are used to accommodate the large number of stitches.

Do not join; work back and forth in rows.

Markers are used to indicate patt reps. Slip markers on each row.

Instructions:

Cast on 108 sts.

FOUNDATION:

Knit 4 rows. Then work in patt as follows:

Row 1: Knit

Row 2: K4, * place marker, YO twice, K1; YO 3 times, K1; YO 4 times, K1; YO 3 times, K1; YO twice, K6. Rep from * to last 4 sts, place marker, K4.

Row 3: Knit across, dropping all YO's from needle. (Gently tug on dropped sts so that they lie flat.) Slip markers.

Row 4: Knit, pulling on dropped sts across row.

Row 5: Knit.

Row 6: K4, * slip marker, K6; YO twice; K1; YO 3 times; K1; YO 4 times, K1; YO 3 times, K1; YO twice. Rep from * to last 4 sts, slip marker, K4.

Row 7: Rep Row 3.

Row 8: Rep Row 4.

Rep rows 1 though 8 until the afghan measures approximately 50".

End by working Row 4 or 8.

Knit 4 rows. Bind off loosely.

FRINGE:

Follow Single Knot Fringe on page 123. Cut strands 15" long. Use two strands folded in half for each knot. Tie knots evenly spaced across cast-on and bound-off ends of afghan.

103

RAFFISH RAFFIA

Designed by Kathleen Power Johnson

Instructions:

Note: Purse is worked in one piece starting at top.

FIRST SIDE:

With straight needles, cast on 30 sts, leaving a 12" yarn end for joining.

Rows 1 through 10: Work in twisted st st.

Row 11: K10, work 5x5 cable, K10.

Rep Rows 1 through 10 until piece measures 4" ending by working a purl row.

Inc Row 1: Cast on 8 sts, knit to end of row in pattern established in Rows 1 through 10.

Inc Row 2: Cast on 8 sts, work across, working last 8 sts in twisted reverse st st: 46 sts.

Next Row: Cont in pattern stitch, working last 8 sts in twisted reverse st st.

Cont working pattern stitch, working Cable Row every 14th row as follows:

Cable Row: K 18, 5x5 cable, K 18.

BOTTOM:

When purse measures 10½" from initial cast on edge, ending by working a purl row, work bottom 4 turning rows in twisted reverse st st.

SECOND SIDE:

Continuing on 46 sts.

Rows 1 through 13: Work in twisted st st.

Row 14 (cable row): K18, 5x5 cable, K18.

Cont working pattern stitch, working Cable Row every 14th row until 2nd side measures same as first to Inc Row 2.

Time to make: About 15 hours

SIZE:

8½" high x 9" wide without handles

MATERIALS:

Rayon raffia, 200 yds variegated

Note: Photographed model made with Rayon Raffia, Color Coleus.

14" straight knitting needles Size 8 (5 mm) or size required for gauge

Three 8" double-pointed knitting needles size 9 (5.5 mm)

Cable stitch needle or short double-pointed knitting needle

Pair of 5" round plastic purse handles

GAUGE:

18 sts and 20 rows = 4" in Twisted Stockinette Stitch

Note: Slip first stitch of each row to make selvage edge.

SPECIAL STITCHES:

Twisted Stockinette Stitch: Working in the back of each st, * Knit 1 row, purl one row; rep from *.

Twisted Reverse Stockinette Stitch: Work as for twisted stockinette stitch with knit rows on wrong side and purl rows on right side.

5 x 5 Cable Stitch: Slip 5 sts to cable stitch needle and hold in front of work, loosely knit 5 sts, then knit 5 stitches from cable needle.

Next Row: Work last 8 sts in twisted reverse st st.

Dec Row 1: Bind off 8 sts and cont across, working last 8 sts in twisted reverse st.

Dec Row 2: Bind off 8 sts. Work in patt across row: 30 sts.

Work Rows 1 through 11 of First Side until Second Side is the same length as First Side. Bind off, leaving a 12" yarn end for joining.

FINISHING:
Side Seam:

Step 1: Wth right side facing and straight needle, pick up and knit 38 sts along one long side, starting at Inc Row 2 and ending at Dec Row 2 and making certain that there are 19 sts for each side.

Step 2: With one double point needle, K19 sts, with second double point needle, K19 sts.

Step 3: Fold purse in half with wrong side facing and both points next to each other.

Step 4: Insert third double point needle into both fronts of first st on each needle and K2 tog. Rep with second pair of sts.

Step 5: * Pass first st on right-hand needle over second: one st bound off. K next pair of sts tog and bind off.

Rep from * until all sts are bound off.

Rep for other side seam.

BLOCKING:
Place purse between two damp towels for a few hours. Let dry before handling.

ATTACH HANDLES:
Fold 1½" of top over edge of each handle. Pin in place and sew to inside of purse.

SCARF OF MANY STYLES

Designed by Sandy Scoville

Time to make: 8 hours, 30 minutes

SIZE:

12" wide x 60" long

Note: Scarf stretches in both directions;
measurements are approximate.

MATERIALS:

Eyelash yarn, 3 ½ oz red

Note: Photographed model made with
Crystal Palace Fizz, Color #7128 red

Size 13 (9 mm) knitting needles, or size
required for gauge

GAUGE:

3 sts = 1" in Stockinette Stitch (knit one
row, purl one row)

Instructions:

Cast on 3 sts.

Row 1 (right side)**:** Knit.

Row 2: Purl.

Row 3: Inc st in first stitch (knit in front and
back of next st); knit to last st; inc in last st:
5 sts.

Row 4: Purl.

Rows 5 through 36: Rep Rows 3 and 4. At end of Row 36: 37 sts.

Work even in st st until scarf measures about 50". End by working a purl row.

DECREASE ROWS:

Row 1 (right side)**:**

Sl 1 as to knit, K1, PSSO; knit to last 2 sts; K2 tog: 35 sts.

Row 2: Purl.

Rep Rows 1 and 2 until 3 sts rem on needle, ending by working a wrong-side row. Bind off.

Cut two 18" lengths of yarn. Tie a length about 12 inches from each end of scarf.

SPORTY

Designed by Sandy Scoville

Time to make: About 8 hours

SIZE:

Fits up to 21" head

MATERIALS:

Worsted weight yarn, 3 ½"oz red
14" straight knitting needles Size 7
   (4.5 mm), or size required for gauge
Five size 7 (4.5 mm) double-pointed
   needles
Size 16 tapestry needle
Thin plastic or cardboard

GAUGE:

4 sts = 1" in Stockinette Stitch (knit one
row, purl one row)

Instructions:

Brim (make 2): With straight needles, cast
on 45 sts.

Row 1 (right side)**:** Knit.

Row 2: Purl.

Row 3: K2 tog tbl; knit to last 2 sts, K2 tog:
43 sts.

Row 4: Purl.

Rows 5 and 6: Rep Rows 3 and 4. At end
of Row 6: 41 sts..

Rows 7 through 10: Rep Rows 3 and 4
twice. At end of Row 10: 39 sts.

Row 11: Rep Row 3. At
end of row: 37 sts.

Row 12: P2 tog; purl
to last 2 sts, P2 tog tbl:
35 sts.

Rows 13 through 16:
Rep Rows 11 and 12
twice. At end of Row 16:
27 sts.

Row 17: Rep Row 11.
At end of row: 25 sts.

Bind-off Row: P2 tog;
bind off all sts to last 2 sts;
P2 tog tbl; finish off.

Trace one brim piece
onto plastic or cardboard.
Cut out.

Holding brim pieces with
right sides tog; sew leaving cast-on rows
open. Turn right-side out.

Insert cut plastic or cardboard; sew cast-on
rows tog.

HEADBAND:

With double-pointed needles, cast on 20 sts
on each of 4 needles: 80 sts; join, work
in rnds.

Rnds 1 through 5: Knit.

Rnd 6 (turning row)**:** Purl.

Rnds 7 through 12: Knit. Bind off all sts.

With wrong sides tog, fold headband at
turning row. Carefully matching sts, sew
tog with overcast st.

BODY:

First Section:

Row 1: Hold headband with turning row at
top; with straight needles, and working in
one exposed lp of each st on turning row,

108

pick up and knit 10 sts. Turn, leaving rem st unworked.

Row 2: Purl.

Row 3: Inc (knit in front and back of next st); knit 8, inc: 12 sts.

Row 4: Purl.

Row 5: Inc; K10, inc: 14 sts.

Row 6: Purl.

Row 7: Knit.

Row 8: Purl.

Rows 9 through 20: Rep Rows 7 and 8.

Row 21: K2 tog tbl; knit to last 2 sts; K2 tog: 12 sts.

Row 22: Purl.

Rows 23 through 30: Rep Rows 21 and 22. At end of Row 30: 4 sts.

Row 31: K2 tog tbl; K2 tog: 2 sts.

Row 32: P2 tog. Cut yarn, leaving a 12" end for sewing.

Thread end into tapestry needle and weave through rem 2 sts, removing needles and drawing yarn tight. Weave in end on wrong side.

Second Section:
Row 1: Working on turning rnd of headband to left of first section, pick up and knit 10 sts.

Rows 2 through 32: Rep Rows 2 through 32 of first section.

Third through Eighth Sections:
Work same as second section.

FINISHING:
With tapestry needle and long ends, and carefully matching sts, sew sections together. Sew brim to lower edge of headband.

ELEGANT BEADED SCARF

Designed by Carol Wilson Mansfield

Time to make: About 14 hours

SIZE:

9" x 73"

MATERIALS:

Novelty printed worsted weight yarn, 4 ozs

Note: *Photographed model made with Crystal Palace Waikiki, Color #3852 Brickyard.*

Size 10 (6 mm) knitting needles or size required for gauge

60 small round glittery beads, multicolor beading needle

GAUGE:

9 sts = 2"

Instructions:

Cast on 38 sts and knit two rows for foundation.

Row 1: K8; * K2 tog, YO, K1, YO; sl 1, K1, PSSO*; K12; rep from * to * once; K8.

Row 2 (and all even rows)**:** K2, working each YO as a st, purl to last 2 sts, K2.

Row 3: K7; * K2 tog, YO, K3, YO; sl 1, K1, PSSO*; K10; rep from * to * once, K7.

Row 5: K6; * K2 tog, YO, K5, YO; sl 1, K1, PSSO*; K8, rep from * to * once, K6.

Row 7: K5; * K2 tog, YO, K7, YO; sl 1, K1, PSSO*; K6, rep from * to * once, K5.

Row 9: K4; * K2 tog, YO, K9, YO; sl 1, K1, PSSO*; K4, rep from * to *, K4.

Row 11: K3; * K2 tog, YO, K11, YO; sl 1, K1, PSSO*; K2, rep from * to *, K3.

Row 13: Rep Row 9.

Row 15: Rep Row 7.

Row 17: Rep Row 5.

Row 19: Rep Row 3.

Row 20: Rep Row 2.

Rep Rows 1 through 20 until scarf measures about 72" long, ending by working a Row 2.

Knit two rows, then bind off loosely. Weave in ends.

FRINGE:

Following Fringe instructions on page 123, cut two 12" long strands of yarn for each knot. Thread each length into beading needle, add beads as desired, alternating placement and knotting yarn below each bead. Tie knots at each outer edge and every third st across each short end.

BEAUTIFUL IN BRONZE

Designed by Sandy Scoville

Time to make: About 5 hours.

SIZE:

About 15" long x 44" wide

Note: *Hip Scarf is stretchy. Lay flat to measure.*

MATERIALS:

Ribbon-type yarn, 261 yds, bronze

Note: *Photographed model made with Crystal Palace Yarns Glam, Color #1997 Chestnut/Copper.*

24" circular knitting needle, Size 10 (6 mm), or size required for gauge

Size H (5 mm) crochet hook

Size 18 tapestry needle

30 gold spaghetti beads, 6mm x 9mm

One gold buckle, 1" (25mm) wide

Tacky glue

GAUGE:

7 sts = 2" in Garter Stitch (knit every row)

Instructions

Cast on 3 sts; do not join. Work back and forth in rows.

Row 1 (right side)**:** Inc (knit in front and back of first st), K1, inc: 5 sts.

Row 2: Inc; K3, inc: 7 sts.

Rep Row 2 until scarf measures about 44" wide when slightly stretched.

Bind off loosely.

FINISHING:

Step 1: Cut 15, 12" strands of yarn. Mark random placement of 11 fringes. With crochet hook, carefully draw strands through selected stitches and knot, having all ends on right side of Hip Scarf.

Step 2: Slip one bead onto each strand end; tie knot in end. Glue to hold in place; trim ends below knot.

Step 3: With crochet hook, attach remaining 4 strands to one end of buckle; attach beads as in step 2.

Step 4: To wear on hips: wrap scarf around you; slip ends into buckle, one at a time and carefully draw in to fit.

SNAPPY SCRAPPY PURSE

Designed by Sandy Scoville

Time to make: About 12 hours

SIZE:

8 1/2" wide x 9 1/2" high

MATERIALS:

Worsted weight yarn, 2 oz tan; worsted
weight chenille yarn, 1 oz rust; eyelash-
type yarn, 100 yds lt tan; bulky weight
chenille yarn, 3 oz brown

Note: *Photographed model made with
TLC® Amore™, Color# 3003, Sand;
Crystal Palace Cotton Chenille, Color
#5137, rust; Crystal Palace Fizz, Color
#7322, camel; and Lion Brand Chenille
Thick and Quick®, Color #227
Desert Print.*

Size 7 (4.5 mm) knitting needles, or size
required for gauge

Two size 7 (4.5 mm) double-pointed
needles

Size H (5.5mm) crochet hook
One 5/8" decorative button
Size 16 tapestry needle

GAUGE:

With tan and eyelash held together,
4 sts = 1" in Stockinette Stitch (knit one
row, purl one row)

Instructions

BACK

With tan and eyelash held together,
cast on 33 sts.

Row 1 (right side)**:** Purl.

Row 2: Knit.

Row 3: Knit.

Row 4: Purl.

Rows 5 through 14: Rep Rows 3 and 4.

Join brown, carry tan and eyelash along
side edge.

Rows 15 and 16: With brown, knit. Cut
brown.

Rows 17 and 18: With tan and eyelash,
rep Rows 3 and 4.

Join rust, carry tan along side edge.

Rows 19 through 26: With rust and eyelash held together, rep Rows 3 and 4. Cut
rust.

Rows 27 and 28: With tan and eyelash,
rep Rows 3 and 4.

Join brown; carry tan and eyelash along
side edge.

Rows 29 and 30: With brown, rep Rows
15 and 16 (garter st ridge). Cut brown.

Rows 31 through 42: With tan and eyelash held together, rep Rows 3 and 4.

Join rust; carry tan along side edge.

Rows 43 and 44: With rust and eyelash
held together, knit. Cut rust.

Rows 45 and 46: With tan and eyelash
held together, rep Rows 3 and 4.

Join brown. Carry tan and eyelash along
side edge.

Row 47: With brown, K2 tog tbl; K 29;
K2 tog: 31 sts.

114

Row 48: Purl.

Rows 49 and 50: Rep Rows 3 and 4. Cut brown.

Row 51: With tan and eyelash held together, inc (knit in front and back of next st); K29; inc: 33 sts.

Row 52: Purl.

Join rust. Carry tan along side edge.

Rows 53 and 54: With rust and eyelash held together, knit. Cut rust.

Rows 55 through 58: With tan and eyelash held together, rep Rows 3 and 4.

FRONT FLAP:

Rows 1 (right side) **and 2:** Purl.

Row 3: Knit.

Rows 4 through 6: Purl.

Row 7: K2 tog tbl; knit to last 2 sts; K2 tog: 31 sts.

Row 8: Purl.

Rows 9 through 34: Rep Rows 7 and 8. At end of Row 34: 5 sts.

Bind off.

FRONT

Work same as back through Row 58.

Bind off as to purl.

FLAP EDGING:

Hold flap with right side facing; with brown, make lp on crochet hook; join with an sc in side of Row 2 of flap; work 14 sc along side edge to Row 34; 2 sc in corner; working along Row 34, sc in next st; sk next st, in next st work (sc, ch 3, sc): button loop made; sk next st, sc in next st, 2 sc in corner, 15 sc along side edge to Row 2 of flap. Finish off.

STRAP:

Note: Strap is worked from right side only - do not turn. Stitches will fold toward the wrong side to form a double-thickness strap.

With double-pointed needles and brown, and leaving an 8" end, cast on 3 sts.

Row 1: Knit. Slide sts to opposite end of needle; do not turn.

Row 2: Carry yarn across wrong side of sts; knit. Slide sts to opposite end of needle; do not turn.

Rep Rows 1 and 2 until strap measures 36". Bind off, leaving an 8" end for sewing.

FINISHING

Step 1: Hold front and back with right sides tog; sew side and bottom seams. Turn right-side out.

Step 2: Fold flap over front and mark for button placement. Sew button to front.

Step 3: Sew strap ends to inside of purse beginning about 2" from top edge at side seams.

JUST ENOUGH TOP

Designed by Sandy Scoville

Note: Instructions are written for size Small; changes for sizes Medium and Large are in parentheses.

Size:	Small	Medium	Large
Body Chest Measurements:	30"–32"	32"–34"	34"–36"
Finished Chest Measurement:	32"	34"	36"

Time to make: About 18 hours

MATERIALS:

Bulky weight ribbon-type yarn, 25 (27, 29) oz sage

Note: Photographed model made with Crystal Palace Yarns Big Net, Color #2141 sage.

14" Size 10½ (6.5 mm) knitting needle, or size required for gauge

Stitch holder

Size I (5.5 mm) crochet hook

GAUGE:

7 sts = 2" in Stockinette Stitch (knit one row, purl one row)

Instructions:

BACK:

Cast on 57 (61, 65) sts.

Row 1 (right side): Knit.

Row 2: Purl.

Rows 3 through 10: Rep Rows 1 and 2.

Row 11 (eyelet row): K1; * YO, K2 tog; rep from * across.

Row 12: Purl, working each YO as a stitch.

Continue in stockinette st until piece measures 10″ from cast-on row, ending by working a purl row.

ARMHOLE SHAPING:

Row 1 (right side)**:** Bind off 3 sts; knit across.

Row 2: Bind off 3 sts; purl across: 51 (55, 59) sts.

Continue in st st until armhole measures 5″ (5 1/2″, 6″).

LEFT BACK NECKLINE AND SHOULDER SHAPING:

Row 1 (right side)**:** K13 (14, 15), slip sts just knit onto stitch holder for right back shoulder; bind off next 25 (27, 29) sts; K13 (14, 15).

Row 2: Purl.

Row 3: K2 tog tbl; knit across: 12 (13, 14) sts.

Row 4: Purl.

Rows 5 through 8: Rep Rows 3 and 4. At end of Row 8: 10 (11, 12) sts.

Work even until armhole measures 7 1/2″ (8″, 8 1/2″). Bind off.

RIGHT BACK NECKLINE AND SHOULDER SHAPING:

Hold back with wrong side facing slip sts from holder onto needle.

Row 1 (wrong side)**:** Purl.

Row 2 (right side)**:** Knit to last 2 sts; K2 tog: 12 (13, 14) sts.

Row 3: Purl.

Rows 4 through 7: Rep Rows 2 and 3. At end of Row 7: 10 (11, 12) sts.

Work even until neckline shaping measures same as right neckline shaping. Bind off.

FRONT:

Work same as back through Row 2 of back armhole shaping.

Continue in St St until armhole measures 4″ (4 1/2″, 5″).

RIGHT FRONT NECKLINE AND SHOULDER SHAPING:

Row 1 (right side)**:** K15 (16, 17), slip sts just knit onto stitch holder for left front shoulder; bind off next 21 (23, 25) sts; K15 (16, 17).

Row 2: Purl.

Row 3: K2 tog tbl; knit across: 14 (15, 16) sts.

Row 4: Purl.

Rows 5 through 12: Rep Rows 3 and 4. At end of Row 12: 10 (11, 12) sts.

Work even until right front measures same as back. Bind off.

LEFT FRONT NECKLINE AND SHOULDER SHAPING:

Hold front with wrong side facing; slip sts from holder onto left-hand needle.

Row 1 (wrong side)**:** Purl.

Row 2 (right side)**:** K13 (14, 15); K2 tog: 14 (15, 16) sts.

Row 3: Purl.

117

continued on page 118

JUST ENOUGH TOP
continued

Rows 4 through 11: Rep Rows 2 and 3. At end of Row 11: 10 (11, 12) sts.

Work even until left front measures same as back. Bind off.

Sew right shoulder seam.

NECKLINE TRIM:
Row 1 (right side)**:** Beginning at last row of left front shoulder, pick up and knit 9 sts along left front shoulder, 21 (23, 25) sts along center front, 9 sts to shoulder seam, 6 sts along right back shoulder, 25 (27, 29) sts along center back, and 6 sts along left back shoulder: 76 (80, 84) sts.

Rows 2 and 3: Knit.

Bind off loosely.

Sew other shoulder seam.

ARMHOLE TRIM:
Row 1 (right side)**:** Hold one armhole with right side facing; working between bound-off sts, pick up and knit 2 sts for every 3 rows.

Rows 2 and 3: Knit.

Bind off loosely.

Repeat for other armhole trim.

FINISHING:
Sew edge of sleeve trims to bound-off sts. Sew side seams.

DRAWSTRING:
With crochet hook, ch 200 sts; sl st in 2nd ch from hook and in each rem ch.

Finish off. Weave in ends.

Beginning and ending at center front, weave chain through eyelet row.

FRINGE:
Cut one 12" yarn length for each stitch across front neckline. With crochet hook, make single knot fringe (see page 123) in each stitch of Row 2 around front neckline. Tie ends of each fringe together. Trim ends.

REFRESHER COURSE IN KNITTING

HOW TO KNIT

CASTING ON

There are many ways to cast on. If you are a beginner, try this easy method. Use only one needle. First, measure a length of yarn that will give you about 1" for each stitch to be cast on. First make a slip knot on the needle; make a yarn loop, leaving about 4" of yarn at the free end; insert the needle into the loop and draw up the yarn from the free end to make a loop on the needle.

Pull the yarn firmly, but not too tightly to form the slip knot on the needle. This slip knot counts as your first stitch.

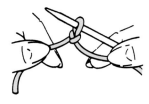

Now begin the casting on:

Step One: Hold the needle with the slip knot in your right hand and with yarn from the skein to your left. With your left hand, make a yarn loop.

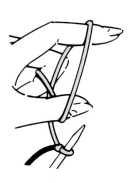

Insert the needle into the loop.

Step Two: Still holding the loop in your left hand, with your right hand, pick up the yarn from the skein and bring it back to front around the needle.

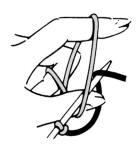

Step Three: Bring the needle through the loop and toward you; at the same time, pull gently on the yarn end to tighten the loop. Make it snug but not tight below the needle.

You have now cast on one stitch. Repeat Steps 1 through 3 for each additional stitch required.

THE KNIT STITCH

Step One: Hold the needle with the cast-on stitches in your left hand. Insert the point of the right needle into the first stitch, from right to left.

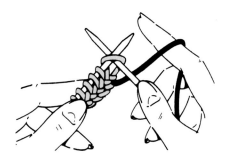

Step Two: With right index finger, bring the yarn under and over the point of the right needle.

Step Three: Draw the yarn through the stitch with the right needle point.

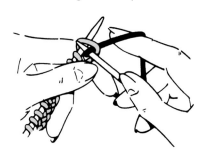

Step Four: Slip the loop on the left needle off, so the new stitch is entirely on the right needle.

You have now made one complete knit stitch.

THE PURL STITCH

The purl stitch is actually the reverse of the knit stitch. Instead of inserting the right needle point from left to right under the left needle (as you did for the knit stitch), you now insert it from right to left, in front of the left needle.

Step One: Insert the right needle from right to left, into the first stitch and in front of the left needle,

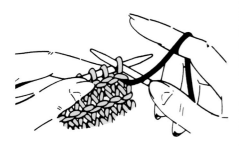

Step Two: Holding the yarn in front of the work (side toward you), bring it around the right needle counterclockwise.

Step Three: With right needle, pull the yarn back through the stitch.

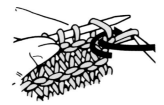

Step Four: Slide the stitch off the left needle, leaving the new stitch on the right needle.

You have now made one complete purl stitch.

BINDING OFF

When a piece is finished, you need to get it off the needles. This is called binding off, and here is how to do it.

To bind off on the knit side:

Step One: Knit the first 2 stitches. Now insert the left needle into the first of the 2 stitches.

Pull the first stitch over the second stitch and completely off the needle. You have now bound off one stitch.

Step Two: Knit one more stitch; insert left needle into the first stitch on the right needle and pull it over the new stitch and completely off the needle. Another stitch is now bound off.

Repeat Step Two until all the stitches are bound off and one loop remains on the right-hand needle. Now to "finish off" or "end off" the yarn, cut it and draw through the last loop,

To bind off on the purl side

Step One: Purl the first 2 stitches. Now insert the left needle into the first stitch on the right needle, and pull it over the second stitch and completely off the needle. You have now bound off one stitch.

Step Two: Purl one more stitch; insert the left needle into the first stitch on the right needle and pull it over the new stitch and completely off the needle. Another stitch is bound off.

Repeat Step Two until all stitches are bound off; then finish off.

YARN OVER

To make a yarn over (an extra lp on needle) before a knit stitch:

Bring the yarn to the front of the work as if you were going to purl, then take it over the right needle to the back into the position for knitting; then knit the next stitch.

To make a yarn over before a purl stitch

Bring the yarn around the right needle from front to back, then back around into position for purling; purl the next stitch

INCREASING

Increasing is a shaping technique in which stitches are added, making the knitted piece wider. The most commonly used method to work an increase is to knit (or purl) twice into the same stitch.

To increase in a knit stitch

Step One: Insert the tip of right needle into the stitch from front to back as to knit; now knit the stitch in the usual manner but don't remove the stitch from the left needle.

Step Two: Insert the right needle (from front to back) into the back loop of the same stitch, and knit it again, this time slipping the stitch off the left needle.

You have now increased one stitch.

To increase in a purl stitch

Step One: Insert the right needle into the stitch from back to front as to purl; now purl the stitch in the usual manner but don't remove the stitch from the left needle.

Step Two: Insert the right needle (from back to front) into the back loop of the same stitch and purl it again, this time slipping the stitch off the left needle.

You have now increased one stitch.

Another method for increasing stitches is called "yarn over" and is used for a decorative increase. This method should only be used when it is called for in the pattern as it leaves a small decorative hole in the work.

Yarn over between 2 knit stitches

Bring the yarn to the front of the work as if you were going to purl, then take it over the right needle to the back of the work. Yarn is now in position to knit the next stitch, and you have added one stitch.

Yarn over between 2 purl stitches

Bring the yarn over the right needle to the back of the work, then bring the yarn forward between the needles to the front of the work. The yarn is now in position to purl the next stitch, and you have added one stitch.

DECREASING

Decreasing is another shaping technique in which stitches are removed, making the knitted piece narrower. The first method of decreasing most commonly used is knitting or purling two stitches together and is worked simply by knitting (or purling) 2 stitches as one.

To knit 2 stitches together

This method, abbreviated K2 tog, is worked by inserting the right needle through the fronts of the first 2 stitches on the left needle as if to knit

Then knit these 2 stitches as one, and you have decreased one stitch.

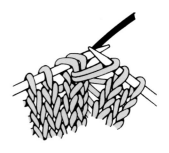

To purl 2 stitches together

This method abbreviated, P2 tog, is worked by inserting the right needle through the fronts of the next 2 stitches on the left needle as to purl. Then purl these 2 stitches as one, and you have decreased one stitch.

Passing the slipped stitch over, abbreviated PSSO, is the second most commonly used method for decreasing. It is often used in shaping where a definite decrease line is desired. The action of slipping a stitch transfers a stitch from the left needle to the right needle without working it.

To slip a stitch as to knit

Insert the right needle into the stitch on the left needle as if you were going to knit it. Instead of knitting, slip the stitch from the left needle to the right needle.

To slip a stitch as to purl

Insert the right needle into the stitch on the left needle as if you were going to purl it. Instead of purling, slip the stitch from the left needle to the right needle.

Note: Always slip a stitch as to knit unless otherwise specified in instructions

To work PSSO

Slip the next stitch as to knit; then knit the next stitch. Pass the slipped stitch over the knitted stitch by using the point of the left needle to lift the slipped stitch over the knitted stitch as in binding off.

WEAVING IN ENDS

When you finish your project, all of the yarn ends should be woven in securely. To do this, use a size 16 tapestry needle or a plastic yarn needle and weave the yarn ends through the backs of the stitches, first weaving about 2" in one direction and then 1" in the reverse direction. Cut off excess yarn.

GAUGE

This is probably the most important aspect of knitting!

GAUGE simply means the number of stitches per inch, and the number of rows per inch that result from a specified yarn worked with needles in a specified size. But since everyone knits differently-some loosely, some tightly, some in-between-the measurements of individual work can vary greatly, even when the knitters use the same pattern and the same size yarn and needles.

If you don't work to the gauge specified in the pattern, your knitted projects will never be the correct size, and you may not have enough yarn to finish your project.

Needle sizes given in instructions are merely guides, and should never be used without making a 4" square sample swatch to check your gauge. It is your reponsiblity to make sure you achieve the gauge specified in the pattern.

To achieve the gauge specified, you may need to use a different needle size-either larger or smaller-than that specified in the pattern. If you have more stitches or rows per inch than specified, you will have to try a size larger needle. If you have fewer stitches or rows per inch than specified, you will have to try a size smaller needle. Always change to larger or smaller needles if necessary to achieve gauge.

FRINGE

Basic Instructions

Cut a piece of cardboard about 6" wide and half as long as specified in the instructions for strands plus ½" for trimming allowance. Wind the yarn loosely and evenly lengthwise around cardboard. When the card is filled, cut the yarn across one end. Do this several times; then begin fringing. You can wind additional strands as you need them.

Single Knot Fringe

Hold the specified number of strands for one knot of fringe together, then fold in half.

Hold the knitted project with the right side facing you. Using a crochet hook, draw the folded ends through the space or stitch from right to wrong side.

Pull the loose ends through the folded section.

Draw the knot up firmly.

Space the knots as indicated in the pattern instructions. Trim the ends of the fringe evenly.

CROCHETING

Crochet is often used as a finishing technique on knitted garments.

To start, make a slip knot on the hook, leaving a 4" yarn tail

Join by pulling the yarn through the specified knit stitch and through the loop on the hook.

To make a chain stitch (ch): YO hook from back to front, hook yarn and draw through the loop on the hook. One chain stitch made.

To work a single crochet stitch (sc)

Step 1: YO hook from back to front, and draw through the 2 loops on the hook

Step 2: Hook the yarn and draw through the 2 loops: one single crochet made.

MAKING TASSELS

Cut a piece of cardboard about 6" wide and the desired length of the finished tassel. Wind the yarn around the length of cardboard the number of times necessary to make the desired tassel. Cut a piece of yarn about 20" long, and thread into a tapestry needle doubled. Insert the needle through all strands at the top of the cardboard, pull up tightly and knot securely, leaving ends for attaching to the garment. Cut the yarn at the opposite end of the cardboard, and remove the cardboard.

Cut another strand of yarn 12" long and wrap it tightly twice around the tassel approximately 1½" below the top knot. Knot securely and allow excess ends to fall in as part of the tassel.

KNITTING NEEDLES CONVERSION CHART

U.S.	0	1	2	3	4	5	6	7	8	9	10	10½	11	13	15	17
METRIC	2	2.25	2.75	3.25	3.5	3.75	4	4.5	5	5.5	6	6.5	8	9	10	12.75

ABBREVIATIONS AND SYMBOLS

Knitting patterns are written in a special shorthand, which is used so that instructions don't take up too much space. They sometimes seem confusing, but once you learn them, you'll have no trouble following them.

These are standard abbreviations

beg . . . . beginning
BO . . . . bind off
CO . . . . cast on
ch . . . . chain
dec . . . . decrease
Fig. . . . . figure
inc. increase(ing)
K . . . . knit
lp(s) . . . . loop(s)
P . . . . purl
patt. pattern
prev. previous
PSSO . . . . pass the slipped stitch over
rem . . . . remain(ing)
rnd(s) . . . . round(s)
rep. repeat(ing)
sc . . . . single crochet
sk. . . . . skip
sl. . . . . slip
sp(s) . . . . space(s)
st(s). . . . . stitch(es)
stock st. . . . . stockinette stitch
tbl . . . . through back loop
tog . . . . together
YO . . . . yarn over the needle

These are standard symbols

* An asterisk (or double asterisks******) in a pattern row, indicates a portion of instructions to be used more than once. For instance, "rep from* three times" means that after working the instructions once, you must work them again three times for a total of 4 times in all.

† A dagger (or double daggers ††) indicates those instructions that will be repeated again later in the same row or round.

: The number after a colon tells you the number of stiches you will have when you have completed the row or round.

( ) Parentheses enclose instructions which are to be worked the number of times following the parentheses. For instance, "(K1, P2) 3 times" means that you knit one stitch and then purl two stitches, three times.

[ ] Brackets and **( )** parentheses are also used to give you additional information, for instance [rem sts are left unworked].

These are standard terms

Finish Off – This means to end your piece by pulling the yarn through the last loop remaining on the needle. This will prevent the work from unraveling.

Work Even – This means that the work is continued in the pattern as established without increasing or decreasing.

Continue in Pattern as Established – This means to follow the pattern stitch as it has been set up, working any increases or decreases in such a way that the established pattern remains the same as it was established.

Right Side – This means the side of the garment that will be seen.

Wrong Side – This means the side of the garment that is inside when the garment is worn.

Right Front – This means the part of the garment that will be worn on the right side of the body

Left Front – This means the part of the garment that will be worn on the left side of the body

---

The patterns in this book have been written using the knitting and crochet terminology that is used in the United States. Terms which may have different equivalents in other parts of the world are listed below

United States	International
Single crochet (sc)	double crochet (dc)
Slip stitch (sl st)	single crochet
Skip	miss
Gauge	tension
Yarn over (YO) . . . . Yarn forward (yfwd) or Yarn around needle (yrn)	

Judith Brossart, Editor

Carol Wilson Mansfield, Art Director

James Jaeger, Photography

Graphic Solutions, inc-chgo, Book Design

All of the garments and projects in this book were tested to ensure the accuracy and clarity of the instructions. We are grateful to the following pattern testers:

Denise Black

Linda Bushey

Kathleen Power Johnson

Carol Wilson Mansfield

Sandy Scoville

Susie Adams Steele

We also extend thanks and appreciation to these contributing designers:

Kathleen Power Johnson

Carol Wilson Mansfield

Sandy Scoville

Susie Adams Steele

Whenever we have used a specialty yarn, we have given the brand name. If you are unable to find these yarns locally, write to the following manufacturers who will be able to tell you where to purchase their products, or consult their internet sites. We also wish to thank these companies for supplying yarn for this book:

Bernat Yarns
320 Livingston Avenue South
Listowel, Ontario
Canada N4W 3H3
www.bernat.com

Crystal Palace Yarns
2320 Bissell Avenue
Richmond, California 94804
www.straw.com

Judi and Company
18 Gallatin Drive
Dix Hills, New York 11746
www.judiandco.com

Lion Brand Yarn Company
34 West 15th Street
New York, New York 10011
www.LionBrand.com

Patons Yarns
320 Lvingstone Avenue South
Listowel, Ontario
Canada N4Q 3H3
www.patonsyarns.com

Red Heart Yarns
Coats and Clark
Consumer Services
P.O.Box 12229
Greenville, South Carolina 29612-0229

TLC Yarns
Coats and Clark
Consumer Services
P.O.Box 12229
Greenville, South Carolina 29612-0229
www.coatsandclark.com

Every effort has been made to ensure the accuracy of these instructions.
We cannot be responsible for human error or variations in your work.

INDEX (bold face entries indicate pattern pages)

continued on page 128

INDEX

continued